THE FLIGHT

MY OPIOID JOURNEY

CAMMIE WOLF RICE

WITH DENNIS ROSS

BOOKLOGIX
Alpharetta, GA

The medical information provided by Christopher Wolf Crusade, in the absence of a visit with a healthcare professional, must be considered as an educational service only. The information provided should not be relied upon as a medical consultation. This mechanism is not designed to replace a physician's independent judgment about the appropriateness or risks for a given patient.

Many external links have been provided on this site as a service and convenience to our users. These external sites are created and maintained by other public and private organizations. We do not control or guarantee the accuracy, relevance, timeliness, or completeness of this outside information.

ISBN: 978-1-6653-0494-8 - Hardcover
ISBN: 978-1-6653-0495-5 - Paperback
eISBN: 978-1-6653-0496-2 - ePub

These ISBNs are the property of BookLogix for the express purpose of sales and distribution of this title. The content of this book is the property of the copyright holder only. BookLogix does not hold any ownership of the content of this book and is not liable in any way for the materials contained within. The views and opinions expressed in this book are the property of the Author/Copyright holder, and do not necessarily reflect those of BookLogix.

Library of Congress Control Number:

Printed in the United States of America   0 7 1 3 2 2

♾ This paper meets the requirements of ANSI/NISO Z39.48-1992 (Permanence of Paper)

Cover art design by David Browning - Brownsville Creative
Typesetting and interior design by Emily Fritz

THE FLIGHT

MY OPIOID JOURNEY

CAMMIE WOLF RICE
WITH DENNIS ROSS

CONTENTS

1

THE CONNECTION

One day, God decided to launch an airline. Every city will be serviced, every airport is convenient. You can fly anywhere your heart desires, and while you may not arrive on schedule, you will always arrive on time. There's one thing that separates God's airline from its commercial competitors. Every ticket is free, but it will cost you everything.

Service is exceptional. The staff attends to your every need. In fact, they know what you need before you ask. "Overwhelm each passenger with kindness" is their motto. The people you meet, and the conversations you have, remain with you for a lifetime. The passenger list is a beautiful mosaic. Next to you may be a corporate CEO, and next to him a homeless man. Right across the aisle may be a nun, and next to her an atheist. God never discriminates. All are welcome, even those who don't believe. But while the people are different, the purpose for their journey is exactly the same.

This airline wasn't built to safely deliver you to your destination. This airline was built to transport you to your purpose. This airline was built to take you places you would never go alone. On each flight, right after the safety announcements, the flight attendant draws your attention to the front as she reads a message for your journey.

"Ladies and gentlemen, welcome to Heavenly Airlines. You are here because you have somewhere to go. You are here because you have something to accomplish far beyond the plans you've made for your own life. This trip will not be easy. There is great turbulence ahead. At times, you will feel as if everything is falling apart. You will reach for someone to hold onto and find no one there. At times, you will want to get off and try things on your own, but let me assure you, your pain is by design and your survival is guaranteed. Just when you want to give up, Heavenly Airlines has one word of encouragement — don't."

This announcement causes a bit of a stir among the passengers. Most of whom weren't expecting philosophical flight instructions. People begin to mumble, trying to figure out where each is from and what brought them to this journey with God. One woman turns to the man beside her and asks, "What made you take this flight today?"

The man looks up with tears threatening to fall and says, "I have three months to live." The stranger grips the hand of the woman, squeezing it as a sign of instant understanding.

Another man wearing a thick, multilayered purple coat leans across the aisle and asks the man sitting in stoic composure the same question, "What brings you here?" he asks.

"Lost my entire family in a fire," the man replies. Slowly, he retreats from the aisle in respect, bows his head and resettles in his seat. Others on the flight have no such tragedies. There is a soccer team in the back heading to a tournament, a newlywed couple heading to their honeymoon and even a grandmother traveling to see her new grandchild. It is a mixed bag. I was in seat 2-A.

This was my first flight, well, my first of this kind. I spent a large part of my life on commercial flights I didn't want to take. Obligations and opportunities can place you thirty thousand feet in the air when just hours before you were relaxing at home. Everything can be calm, and suddenly things change.

Normally, when I travel, I would take all the things a girl needs. In other words, I take everything. A ten-day trip needs twenty days' worth of clothes. It's just the way it is. A lady has to prepare for weather, formal and informal gatherings, unexpected meetings, the mountains, the valleys and the beach, even if the place you are going has none of these. Most of my packing never got unpacked, as most of what I would bring would never be touched, but there is comfort in excess. However, there was something different about taking this flight with God. There were certain rules against boarding with things you don't need.

Rule number one was to travel light. Passengers must take only what is absolutely necessary for the time they plan to be gone. Any delays, any modifications to their schedule, should never cause one to worry. Heavenly Airlines guarantees each person will receive what they need at the moment they need it. Shoes, clothes, coats and jackets are all provided should a passenger find themself in a bind, which brings me to another unique point about this airline. There are many unscheduled stops.

Some stops last for days, some for months, some for years. You never know where Heavenly Airlines will take you, all you know is you will arrive at your destination on time.

The unscheduled stops are well known. There is a city called "Joy," one called "Happiness," "Success and Wealth" are favorite stops, but there are also places no one wants to go, places like Disappointment, Despair, Sickness, and Poverty. Forgiveness can be a difficult stop, so can Reconciliation, but the hardest of them all is a city called Grief. There is no way you can know where you'll be at any given moment. You just know that what surprises you never surprises God. Your trip has been well-planned.

As for me, I needed more information about what to expect. I gathered from listening to the conversations around me that everyone wasn't new. While this was my first rodeo, there were some veterans on board.

In my mind, the more you fly, the more you come to understand the airline. Each trip becomes less and less mystifying. Each trip grows in meaning and understanding. I was nervous, but I turned around and asked a handsome gentleman sitting behind me if there was any advice he could give. He smiled and said, "Always remember who owns the airline."

I wasn't totally sure what he meant and so I asked for more clarity. "What do you mean, sir?"

"I've been taking these flights for a while, started back in college," he said. "There were times I tried to take matters into my own hands and guide them the way I thought they should go. There was a period when I thought I knew what was best. The reality is, I had forgotten who owns this airline. This is not a normal journey; this is a spiritual journey with an earthly connection. Just like flying from Los Angeles to Miami may have a connection in Atlanta, this journey is flying from eternity to eternity, and it connects on earth. Never forget that. Earth is a connection, not a destination. Some are here longer than others, but it is still only a connection. You will get to the place you are supposed to go. The owner will make sure of it."

I didn't really know how to respond. His words hit me at a place I didn't know I had. Everything he said was confusing and made sense all at the same time. As I was thinking about what he said, he introduced himself.

"I'm Ted."

"Nice to meet you, Ted. I'm Cammie."

I sat back in my seat. This was going to be an experience. *What did he mean with the connection comment?* It sounded a bit like the philosophical advice given by the flight attendant earlier. *Was I even in the right place? How did I get here?*

There were magazines in the pocket in front of me. I pulled one out and began to read more about Heavenly Airlines. One paragraph under the heading, *Who We Are,* caught my attention. It read, "Some chose to fly with us, but most are chosen. You may start off alone or with traveling companions — but those who start the journey with you may not be with you in the end. Many decide to stay at different stops along the way. You will meet new people on your travels, new relationships will form, old ones may fade. The place a plane touches down may be your friend's final destination, but you may still have a way to go to reach your place of purpose."

I couldn't get the connection comment out of my mind. It felt like understanding that one point was going to bring me a level of understanding that I otherwise would not have. My mind began to wander off, as I stared at the ceiling of the plane. Everything was purple. The recessed lighting, the doorknobs, the carpet and even the branded wool covers to keep our legs warm. Everything.

Right then, the cry of a child broke through my thoughts. The baby couldn't have been more than two or three. Somehow, the crying calmed me down. It seemed to be one of the few normal sounds I'd heard all day. I'm sure the little one was tired, hungry or needed to be changed. Either way, it was something I understood, something that made me feel like everything wasn't foreign. The mother tried to quiet the child.

"Bodhi, Bodhi," she called. "Go to sleep."

I turned around to find where the voice was coming from. Tiny feet were sticking out of the aisle about twenty rows behind me. We started taxiing down the runway about to take off. The lights went low.

"Please fasten your seatbelts," came over the speakers.

Mine was already tight, but I tightened it more.

Why did the flight attendant say this flight would be turbulent? I thought. *Every flight I've ever taken had some rough spots. Why would she make it a point to bring up the obvious?* My mind was racing.

We started down the runway, picking up speed at a rate I don't recall ever experiencing. Halfway down and we were going so fast, I was wondering why we weren't in the air yet.

Bells began to ring, and a purple light came on.

I looked around to find Ted. With my eyes, I asked, *What's going on?*

He smiled and nodded.

I gripped the partition between my seat and the next. White knuckled.

The plane began shaking uncontrollably.

We tried to get up in the air but slammed back to the runway.

Luggage burst out from the overhead, falling to the floor.

One lady screamed, joining the baby's cries.

"Oh my God! What is going on?" I said.

Something is wrong.

The end of the runway is quickly approaching.

I shut my eyes and arched my head to the ceiling.

Why aren't we in the air! I thought.

"Cammie, Cammie."

Huh? Who is calling my name?

The plane vibrates violently, sliding left to right.

We aren't going to make it.

The voice comes in again, louder this time.

"Cammie! Cammie!"

I open my eyes to find my brother standing over me, his hands around my shoulders.

I'm in my parents' home in Bloomington, Indiana. We stare at each other without blinking.

"What's wrong?" he asks. "Did you have a bad dream?"

SCAN HERE FOR MORE

2

THE FLIGHT PLAN

Life can be a dream or a nightmare. The only difference between the two is your perspective. Life can take you to the edge and then push you from behind. Whether we fall to our death or fly toward our purpose depends on who we believe is in control of our journey.

It is difficult to express in words what pierces the heart. Our most debilitating experiences sit inside of us, wordless. There is no language down there. There are no catchphrases that accurately point others to the spot bleeding in our very soul. We are left with vanilla expressions to describe a colorful pain. However, I found a workaround.

Fiction is the greatest cover for truth. Imagination has no rules. Ironically, neither does pain. Together, this *ruleless* pair creates the greatest tool for freeing ourselves from an existence full of quiet suffering. Imagine and be free.

After you live a while, a few things become clear. Things you thought mattered may not, and things you didn't pay much attention to can be critically important. People we once called friends may actually be enablers of our destruction, while others we think are against us may be opposing our actions for our own good. It all depends on who we think controls our journey.

If you could see me right now, you would notice my hands are shaking. I'm nervous about what I'm about to say. Please bear with me.

When I decided to write this book, I found myself stuck between my future and my past. It can be overwhelming to talk about things I'm not proud of, things that, for years, have lived comfortably in the silence of my soul. It is dangerous to wake up secrets. A lot can go wrong. People can be hurt. However, writing this book demanded honesty, and honesty requires I show my full self.

My life today is so much different from what it was three decades ago. Today, my schedule is filled with high-powered meetings with physicians, businesspersons, and even celebrities. God blesses my family with resources we never had growing up. I travel the world, and there is nothing I want for, but I'm still embarrassed.

I'm embarrassed that I didn't finish college. I'm embarrassed that I failed at marriages. At night, heaven must double as a comedy club, because God surely has a sense of humor. Sometimes, the least qualified person is picked to lead the most qualified geniuses. The only way I can make sense of it all is I assume having to fight through tragedy teaches you a few valuable lessons worthy of sharing with others. Heaven knows I've had to fight.

We can spend our entire lives in hiding, never revealing the losses we endure. We hide without realizing that life doesn't start until we stand emotionally naked in the sunlight for all the world to see. Truth is funny. I say this because, by the time you get the courage to tell your whole story, you find out so many people have been waiting their entire lives to tell theirs. They just need somebody to go first. No more hiding for me. It's my turn to stand in the sun.

I am learning that great wisdom only comes after great mistakes. I am learning that no one finds peace without first having conflict. I would have really appreciated an easier path, but the pilot of my journey filed a different flight plan. The pilot of my journey has decided to take me through mountains and valleys, through struggles and success, and the knowledge gained along the way is worth more than anything money can buy.

My tears allow me to better understand those who cry. Working a dead-end restaurant job as a single mother has allowed me to empathize with mothers who stay afloat because a baby at home depends on them, with mothers who, after putting their children to bed, must rush to the bathroom, sit on the toilet, and quietly weep. We even find wisdom in those circumstances because sleepless nights teach you more than a good night's rest ever will.

What I'm really saying is I don't know what you are facing right now. I don't know your flight plan. You may have experienced trauma, sickness, or molestation. The loss of a loved one may have gutted your happiness, and you may believe you will never smile again. Just know this: even though I can't see your face, I am holding your hand. I know what it's like to be in a place so dark, it's velvet; a place filled with so much pain that it seems death would be an upgrade. Be encouraged and hold on. Remember, turbulence never lasts, and without it, we could never fly.

Only as the winds press against our wings do we create enough tension and force to give us lift. When life moves too fast, when you are ambushed by a job loss or a diagnosis, just know you are about to fly. You are about to awaken to the purpose for which you were born. If everything were still, you would never get off the ground. Somewhere in my story, I hope, you'll see your own, and together we can soar. This is my story.

* * *

My imagination started really young. As a child, I imagined my father loved me. While the man who raised me was, and still is, one of the most incredible men I know, there was something missing. I had never met my biological father, and this is my first unscheduled stop — reconciliation.

It was difficult for me to write these words. For one, I never called the man I'm speaking of "father," not once in my life. He is my DNA, not my DAD. Second, I would have never intentionally done anything to hurt my dad. He was with me, my mother and my brother every step of the way. I would never want him to feel he was not a great dad to me. He truly was, and still is. Yet, as I got older, I wanted to know more about myself, and there were some questions only my birth father could answer, like "Why do my hands look like they do?" and, most importantly, "Why did you leave my mother when she needed you most?"

Before I explain the series of random events leading to me meeting my biological father, I have to provide context. I grew up in a small place called Bloomington, Indiana. Don't worry, I won't be offended if you've never heard of it, but it is the home of a great University and basketball team! The Colts and that little car race in Indianapolis take up all the oxygen in the room when you mention Indiana. Growing up in small-town Bloomington was perfect for me. I simply love the place.

All of my family lived in Bloomington. I was known as the bossy kid, but I can explain. I was the oldest of all my cousins, so

I had to run a tight ship among the little ones. I always had to take care of my brother, Roger. He is seven years younger than me. My cousin, Avery, is eight years younger than me. Michelle is two years younger than me. On Sundays, like clockwork, we all went to church, the First Church of God, to be exact. Donald Talley was our pastor. If you were a child in Bloomington, going to church was the fee you had to pay to get to the good part, which was the after-church meal, and there was only one place to go: Ladyman's Cafeteria on 122 E. Kirkwood Avenue.

Ladyman's was straight out of central casting. A small-town gathering place with good food and even better people. The best homemade chicken noodles, legendary pies and everything you could imagine at a small-town restaurant. Based on their clothes, you could see who went to worship that Sunday and who stayed home to cut the lawn instead. The place echoed with laughter and side conversations between friends who hadn't seen each other in a week. We were close-knit. We looked out for each other.

The kids would grab a corner and feast on cream-flavored Dum Dum suckers. No idea where the name came from. Michelle and Avery, along with Roger, and I would have the best time. Life could not have been better.

I was a responsible kid if I do say so myself. I was fiercely independent, but that part came from my mother. Being able to take care of myself was drilled into my head. My mother had a super personality, very loving. Mom became a realtor. She was part of a group of a few women who opened the first all-women Century 21 real estate office in Bloomington. It was a big deal. Years later, mom got her million-dollar real estate pen. Not many women were able to do that back in the '70s. It's something I'm proud of.

Mom's view was if it had to be done, do it yourself. I grew up thinking I didn't need anybody, certainly not a man.

"Cammie, men get a certain age and have a midlife crisis. They're going to have an affair with their secretary, get a sports car, and leave you." That's what my mother would say, over and over. It's a rough thing to tell a young girl.

Looking back, she taught everything out of fear. It's all she knew, so she lived vicariously through me her whole life. I had to do everything she wanted to do. All of it came at a price because, while I got the good stuff, I also ended up making some of the same mistakes my mother made.

In Bloomington, I was like a one-woman Angie's list. If a babysitter was needed to watch the young ones in the neighborhood, I was assigned the task. If the adults were tailgating at a football game or headed out of town to watch the Indianapolis 500, I was left in charge. If we played school, I was the teacher. If we played hospital, I was the doctor. Looking back, I was in leadership training, preparing for a part I was to play much later in my journey. I was a dreamer, and one of my dreams was to be a famous actor one day.

Lights, camera, action! All of it fascinated me. I was in high school when *Breaking Away* was filmed right in our town. I can't tell you how much pride enters a small city when the big trucks and big egos roll into town. Stars like Dennis Quaid were seen in our streets. It was incredible. If I wanted to act before, my passion for the craft only increased once Hollywood showed up.

As a high school student, I would watch movies and imagine myself in them. When I got older, it was Julia Roberts all the way. I loved *Eat Pray Love*. In it, Roberts had everything she wanted in life! But life doesn't tell you where it's going to take you next. Only the pilot knows that. In the movie, she eventually has to figure out what's really important, which launches her into self-discovery.

I used to think the movie was almost a prophecy of what my life would one day be, but now it seems the opposite. I say this because I launched my own self-discovery long before Julia Roberts launched hers on screen. To follow my dreams, I went to California. My plan was to go to acting school, land a few parts, get in a big movie, and become a big star. But I was skipping ahead of my flight plan. I thought my life was on a non-stop trajectory, but the pilot scheduled layovers. There were unresolved issues back home that I would not be allowed to ignore. There was something that happened before I moved to California.

I was a senior in high school. It was a Friday night, and I was home alone. I was casually walking through the kitchen, heading to my room to get dressed and go out, when the phone rang. I looked at it and thought about not answering, but I turned and answered it anyway.

"Hello?"

"Cammie?" a voice said. "It's your father."

3

MY FIRST
UNSCHEDULED STOP

What do you mean you're my father? I thought. My father was not in my life, so there's no way he's on my phone. I was at a loss for words, but the man on the other end, who claimed to be "my father," continued to speak. My real father was Roger Wolf, who lived in my home. I knew his voice and this voice was not his. For the next few minutes, I listened as he expressed a desire to meet me, his daughter; and then things got interesting.

To say this random kitchen call created drama in our home would be an understatement — a nuclear warhead went off, a tsunami, three-mile island. I knew the pain of someone who left my life, but I did not know the pain of their return. It was as if my biological dad had been in space on a NASA voyage since the day I was born, and, on that day, in my senior year of high school, he decided to reenter the earth's atmosphere. Everything began to shake.

When my real dad learned about the phone call, he went ballistic. He wanted to know why this man dared to contact me without first calling him. It was the ultimate disrespect, a violation of "man-law." But, for me — I just needed my questions answered.

I wanted to know who I was, completely. To do this, I had to know more about my biological dad. I needed to know more about the man who helped bring me here. And so, when I graduated from high school, I made up my mind to meet him one day. His name was Hawke. I wouldn't have to wait long because, after graduation, I got word. Hawke was coming to see me.

He was flying to Indiana. The date was set. Back in the day, you could go to the gate and meet someone coming off the plane — no TSA, no throwing away water bottles or taking off your shoes. The day arrived, and I left for the airport to meet the man who only lived in my imagination. I remember standing at the gate, shaking like a wet poodle. Everybody was de-boarding as usual, but, instead of leaving, they moved to the left and the right. I tiptoed through a sea of heads trying to locate a face or a pair of eyes that looked like mine. I found out later that he told everybody on the plane that he was meeting his daughter for the first time — a statement he was proud of when it should have caused him embarrassment.

Five minutes went by. The gate was getting crowded. I'm was getting anxious. The flight attendants walked off. The pilots too. My emotions were everywhere. Certainly, they would not leave a passenger behind. The last thing I needed was for the man who wasn't in my life to stand me up at the airport. I was watching everybody, and then I noticed everybody was watching me. This was crazy! Then there was this extended pause, and in that long gray tunnel connecting the plane to the terminal, a man appeared. He was tall with a smile on his face. That was him. He had my eyes or, more accurately, I had his.

We embraced. Everyone started clapping and cheering like he was a Super Bowl champion. If they only knew. They should probably have cheered that I didn't launch into a tirade, that I didn't scream out a list of important dates he missed, the birthdays, the special times gone forever. I had so many emotions. Hawke, which wasn't his birth name, took me from the airport to this really nice restaurant. I'll never forget it because Adam West, the original Batman, sat a couple of tables over from us. This was a strange day.

When he walked in, everybody was like, "Oh, my God! It's Adam West." I was thinking they should have said, *Oh, my God! Cammie's dad decided to show up in her life!* We sat down and the waiter approached. I was uptight. The tension was peanut butter. Then Hawke said, "We're celebrating! I'd like to make a toast to my new fiancé."

What? I thought.

The joke freaked me out. That's when I learned how much he liked to be funny. Heaven does have a comedy club. It just so happened I wasn't in the funniest of moods. After a few minutes, things calmed a bit. It's difficult to describe what it felt like to see your father as an adult when you never saw him as a child. I didn't know what to say. I didn't know how to feel.

The next day, we went to Brown County in Nashville, Indiana, a place most people have never heard of. We ate biscuits and homemade apple butter. I even caught myself smiling occasionally. I nearly felt guilty for enjoying myself. Hawke didn't deserve my smiles, my laughter, or my presence. He had not earned the right to speak to me, but life is funny like that. Sometimes we must give to others exactly what they never gave to us, and, when we do so, life rewards us with peace. This is a spiritual journey.

This journey assumes several things. It assumes there is a bigger place to go than where we are today. It assumes there will be mountains and valleys. The journey requires a bit of planning, so plan well. Travel lightly, as changes in weather are frequent. Pack a lunch, and boots for the snow. Take enough to survive the lean times. Stay close to those who love you. You never know when you'll need a friend.

This spiritual journey is going to make a demand on you, a demand for honesty, a demand to look difficulties in the face that you've avoided all your life. You'll be forced to speak to people who tear your heart in two. You'll be asked to grant clemency to those who, if given the chance, would send you to the death chair. Such is the journey. It will be as meaningful as you are honest. And there's one more thing to remember: your hardest challenges will come at your weakest moments.

I learned this the hard way. In my life, there were many women I mentored. I told them my story, not because it was so special, but because it could save them years of heartache, years of frustration resulting from years of unforgiveness and misunderstanding. I even had friends ask me why it seemed my life had been full of dysfunction, disappointment, and tragedy. Things happened to me that just didn't seem to happen to anyone else — at least, that's what I thought. Over time, I realized that my stuff is really everybody's stuff; it's just that most people don't talk about their stuff. They'll give you the "cute" conversation. Those on this journey need to hear the ugly one, the one where you don't make all the right decisions, the one where you're not always the hero.

My great-grandparents, Mama and Papa, understood this well. They were the only family members who told me about Hawke. No one else gave me the real story — the ugly one. Mama and Papa looked life straight in the eye. Until then, I made up my own story. That's what happens when you're young: you have a lot of questions, and, the longer they go unanswered, the more questions you have. In the end, meeting Hawke allowed me to move on. It was necessary. It was done. The person who raised me was not the person who physically made me. Meeting him brought clarity. It allowed the sun to shine through. If anything, it made me love the man who adopted me as a child, Roger Wolf Sr., even more. We were thick as thieves. Both my brother, Roger, and I loved him dearly because, in the end, he was the one who never left us.

Mama and Papa deserve so much credit. My life would have been nothing without them. Their love was unconditional. They were perfect in every way. I have so many stories of our relationship, but, for some reason, one stands out. Papa told me that, for many years, he would drive me to middle school every day. He recalled something that took place on our morning drives.

"Cammie," he'd always begin. "I'm driving you to school, and, right before we go around the corner, you look at me and say, 'Papa, slow down. Slow down, Papa! I've got to kiss you *now*. I *can't* kiss you at the school door in front of all my friends.'" Papa slowed down, and I kissed him, the story goes. Like I said, the man was perfect.

I so loved how they decorated their home at Christmastime, how loud it sounded around their kitchen table on Sundays, and how my aunts, uncles and cousins came in and out without announcement. Love was in the air. We were tight knit, living in America's heartland, a family of Hoosiers about as close to a Norman Rockwell painting as a family could be.

Mama's real name was Lillian Carter Raney, my mother's mother's mother. What I lacked in a close relationship with my mother, I more than compensated for with Mama. I was more like Mama than I was like my mother. We were inseparable. She called me "PJ," her Precious Jewel. To this day, I wear her wedding ring.

Mama and Papa owned *Mom & Pop's*, one of Bloomington's landmark restaurants, a go-to place for home-cooked meals — nothing fancy, just hearty, delicious food at affordable prices, something everyone in Indiana appreciates. My great-grandparents were the unofficial mayors of Bloomington. When your best friend is nearly 60 years older, you find yourself doing things other kids don't, things like visiting cemeteries.

That's where I got my love for cemeteries. That is such a weird sentence to write, but it's true. Each Saturday, Mama, Papa and I would rise early, enjoy a hearty *Mom & Pop's* breakfast, and spend the bulk of the day visiting deceased loved ones. We decorated their gravesites with flowers — not exactly Saturday morning cartoons, huh? I loved the peace and serenity, the sense of permanence, the manicured lawns and the community of it all.

We walked the rows, pausing at marble headstones that were all that remained of her many departed relatives. They were *my* many departed relatives, too, she'd always stress. "These are *our people*," she'd say. She would stop at each stone and greet it, excitedly introducing her little PJ to a family member I'd never personally know. She made me understand that death wasn't the end of a relationship.

How lucky I am to have had them! The memories of my *great-grandparents* are vivid and plentiful, which puts me among the most fortunate of people. To know family members three generations older than me is a privilege. The lessons are indelible. Yes, *my great-grandparents* are gone, but that didn't end our relationship. I can see and hear and almost touch them, even now.

It has been years since Mama took her last breath, but I can still smell the Juicy Fruit gum drifting from her purse. I still experience the inner warmth I felt when sleeping on the cool, fatty part of her arm. When I close my eyes, I can see Mama and Papa playing Old Maid with me or buying *waaaay* too much lemonade from my little driveway stand so my business wouldn't go under.

While I was too embarrassed to be seen kissing Papa goodbye at middle school, by high school, I'd blossomed into, as they say in the heartland, an All-American girl. And, in the sports-crazy world of Indiana, that kind of gal is practically *required* to date the quarterback or the green-eyed pitcher with big league dreams and corporate sponsorship written all over him. Enter, Ted.

Ted was all of this rolled into one. He stood six feet, six inches tall with ten feet of handsome — a stud, as they called him. He became my boyfriend in my senior year. Ted was a stand-out center on our high school basketball team. He was offered and accepted an athletic scholarship to Mississippi University while I enrolled in a college far from Bloomington, and moved to Florida.

Anticipating the distance between us could create the usual relationship hardships, we decided to keep ours fun and casual, kind of loose and undefined. Just roll with it, we thought. We took road trips together. We hung out together on breaks — no biggie, no pressure. With Ted, it was a romance that was always light. We had a good thing going. But during one holiday break, my world changed forever.

Ted and I were back in Bloomington from our respective colleges, spending lots of time together. We had a great New Year's Eve and then left to go our separate ways. By mid-January, classes were back in session, and we were back on our respective campuses. By the end of the month, the test confirmed my suspicions: I was pregnant.

I was 20 years old. I broke the news to five of my family members, one by one, and gauged their individual reactions. Mama was worried about what her church friends would think. Others wondered about the neighbors and whether we should try to hide the upcoming baby bump. My dad was stunned, but he knew my position on the issue.

And Papa? Everyone warned me not to tell him. He'd have a heart attack and die on the spot, they said, or his poor heart would break in two. Whatever medical emergency he faced, the news of my pregnancy would trigger a reaction within that would likely wipe him out.

I told him anyway. He was my Papa, after all. Our relationship went back to middle school. Nothing could come between us. Papa's reaction changed everything.

"You're having a baby, Cammie?" he said when I broke the news. There was then a pregnant pause (no pun intended), and then, "You're having a baby, Cammie?! *We're having a baby?! We're having a baby!*" Each phrase rose with excitement. Papa was ecstatic. He jumped up and hugged me and practically danced a jig. He was going to meet his great-great-great-grandbaby, something he'd never imagined possible. It was some kind of miracle he'd lived to see, he said. I kissed him excitedly.

My mother's reaction to the news, though, was less enthusiastic. Her daughter's unplanned, unwed pregnancy from some casual high school crush, that had already reached its expiration date, was a tragedy. I wasn't *ready* for a baby, she said. I needed to get my college degree, and *then* maybe a baby, she tried to explain. I needed to see the *world*, she said, to meet *other* people, to date other guys besides the high school basketball star.

My mom thought my life was over but acted like *her* life was over. She told me I was following in her footsteps — and that wasn't meant as a compliment. She said she'd gotten married too young and her life had been difficult because of it. My life would be hard too, she said. "What about getting a college degree? What will the people at Mama's church think? What about your *future*, Cammie?!" She threw everything but the kitchen sink at me.

When the smoke cleared, she arrived at a conclusion. This was a simple error that needed correcting. "The blackboard needs to be wiped clean," she said, so she offered straightforward advice. It was really a mandate, a command from on high to be carried out, and carried out swiftly. My mother looked me in the eye, and delivered her decision.

SCAN HERE FOR MORE

4

ON OUR OWN

As night gathered around me, I thought about my mother's directive. Bringing a life into the world meant my life was over. She didn't want me to end up like her and marry too young, divorce too soon and fight depression forever, but I had already made up my mind, and the support of Papa only poured concrete over my decision. I was keeping my baby. That was the right decision, but even right decisions can have negative consequences.

To be unmarried and pregnant in Bloomington, Indiana, was like being on the moon without an oxygen tank. You couldn't breathe. The rumors were suffocating. I had a scarlet letter. I was pregnant in a small town where everyone knew everything about everybody. To make things worse, this was right when I was hitting my stride as a young woman. I had just made captain of the dance team at the University of Central Florida and was living on my own in Orlando. My grades were awesome. My future was bright. A baby didn't fit in, but God's plane, or, as most people call it, "God's plan" doesn't always go where we think it's going. And, just like that, overnight, I found myself on a divine detour.

I was a baby having a baby. Yes, I was in college and on my own, but I was not the *adult* I would one day become. I hadn't experienced life to the point that I had enough wisdom to truly go solo. I needed guidance. I needed help in so many areas. My mother knew this, and, even though her advice didn't land well, her intent was pure. It is always complicated when good people give you bad advice. In the end, her love for me was more important than the fact she was wrong.

This was new territory for everyone. I was on a pathway leading to heights few in my family had ever reached. I was in college and doing well. I was going to graduate. "Stay on the path, Cammie," Mom would say. "You have brains and beauty." I wanted to make my mother proud but still have my child. It was another version of *Hoosiers*, our own sequel that never made it to the big screen. Things started changing fast, and I had no idea what was headed my way. I guess my mother did because, even though I made a different decision I was still about to experience marriage, a bad divorce, a second child, a dead-end job, a DJ, a better job, a better marriage, another divorce, and selling tons of Canon color copiers, all before the age of thirty. I know — I can see it in your face. I was confused, too. Stay with me; it will make sense in a moment.

So, Ted and I decided to move back to Bloomington into Ted's parents' basement. While I appreciated having a place to land and prepare for our child, the first thing I learned was basements and pregnancy don't mix — not enough light, not enough ventilation, and the distinct smell of poverty. It didn't take long for me to realize something else: pregnancy was changing my life dramatically but Ted's not so much.

I was a prenatal mess. I dropped out of college and took a job with an emergency call service, which was ironic because I was a living, walking, and breathing emergency myself. I needed to be the one calling the company I worked for. We needed money badly. The baby didn't wait until our savings built up. He wanted out, and, on September 18, 1983, at 8:08 in the morning, Christopher Brett Wolf was born with a head full of beautiful black hair.

With all that was going on around me, his birth brought me much-needed joy. I held him in my arms and watched his eyes look for mine. The feeling is nearly impossible to explain. He was perfect. I needed so much, but, for a moment, nothing mattered. Even his cry was music to my ears. I called him my Zen baby. He brought peace. From the second I saw Christopher, I knew we were going to make it, no matter what. I could not say the same for Ted, and we ended up getting a divorce.

At the time, my parents were living in Sarasota, Florida. I told my mother what was going on, and she said a change of scenery would do us some good. All things considered, it sounded like a decent offer, and, within days, Christopher and I were headed out of Indiana on Interstate 69, a young mother and son in search of a better life. Driving south through endless acres of farmland, I reflected on my decision and its future repercussions, knowing it meant Christopher would likely not grow up near his father.

I had already learned that a child's relationship with their father is equally as important as with their mother. Mothers are so incredible, but there is just something different about the father-child connection. I found this out for myself that day I answered the phone in the kitchen.

It was time to get aggressive. My son would not grow up missing the basics of what a child needed. Even writing about this time in my life these many years later fills me with anxiety.

A mother will do anything, and I do mean *anything*, to care for her child. When I became a mother, life was no longer about me. I dedicated myself to making sure Christopher had everything he needed.

The journey is brutal. We never select for ourselves what God selects for us. That which makes us cry plants seeds of future joy. Those who reject us set the table for later acceptance. Even our mistakes, our unwise decisions, and those events we categorize as regrets all have an irreplaceable role in this turbulent trip called life. No one becomes great by choice; we become great by force. Life forces us onto the tailor-made, fire-burning path that creates character and success. No one willingly steps into the fire any other way.

With Indiana in my rearview mirror, literally and figuratively, we were on our own, but we were not alone. I was confident and scared at the same time. I was determined but confused about what I was going to do. Even in those times, someone was guiding me. There must be prayer fill-ins around the world because I wasn't praying, however, I felt somebody praying — for me.

Once at my parents' place in Sarasota, I started looking for work like my life depended on it, because it did. Every now and then, I would try to take a few hours for myself and go out just to regroup and add balance to an otherwise intensely stressful existence. One night, I went to a local restaurant. It was the hottest nightclub restaurant in town. The owners were from Indiana, so I struck up a conversation about where we were from, and then I lowered the boom and asked for a job. They hired me on the spot.

I started as a server. I loved the relationship I made with my customers. I knew what items on the menu were their favorite and brought them what they needed before they asked. To this day, I have great respect and love for those serving me at restaurants. I see myself in them. Tip your servers well.

Serving got my foot in the door. While working late one night, I heard the manager talking about how they were losing money. This manager basically said the hostess was putting the door money in her pocket. I saw an opening. The next morning, at eight o'clock, I was right there in the owner's face with a decent proposal.

"I can manage this place."

He looked at me with a smirk that said, "You have never managed a restaurant in your entire life, woman." The smirk was right. But I kept pushing.

"I know the ins and outs of this place. I can do it, believe me, I can. I will not let you down."

I don't know if it was to prove me wrong, but I got the job. Game on! I went from server to general manager of the restaurant and the nightclub. I started to make real money. I took good care of Christopher. I met people.

There was one person, in particular, David Browning. David was a DJ hired by the restaurant to increase the party scene at night.

"Who is the hot hostess?" David asked the guy next to him, as he was setting up his music equipment for the evening.

"Uh, well, that's your new boss," the guy said. "She's the general manager."

"No shit?"

"Yep, none."

David was playing music and getting the place going when I walked up and grabbed his cocktail glass.

"You're not drinking on the job, are you?" I asked.

He answered my question with a question of his own. "Who are you?"

That question took many walks and many dinners over many years to answer. Once it was thoroughly answered, David had one more question.

"Will you marry me?"

I said yes. The woman he thought was the hostess, but who was really his boss, over the next few years, eventually became his wife. We had a beautiful son, Chase. My journey continued. The next few years were a serious adjustment period. New town, new job, new husband, new experience, new baby. Christopher had a new sibling, but when you're the star and someone else is added to the show, things can get a little rocky. Christopher had been the total focus for about seven years, and now Chase had been added to the "tour." The opening act wasn't happy.

Christopher was the best child ever. He was always on my hip. I could take him anywhere and do anything with him in tow. He was just mellow, Zen; everything was always great. On the other hand — and we can laugh about it now — my beautiful Chase would give me hell, the holy kind. He was named Chase for a reason. I chased him from the word go. He's like his father, David, a musician, actor and creative soul — and creatives don't like to sit still.

Christopher and Chase were always watching, learning and soaking everything in. When children are young, struggles can be hidden. All they want is food, a warm place to sleep and the love of their mother. Then, as the years go by, they begin to notice they don't have what other kids have. They notice your car isn't as nice as the other parents' cars at school. At least, that's what happens in theory because that wasn't my experience. Christopher rolled with the punches. Good, bad or indifferent, money or no money, he knew how to make me feel like I was the best mother in the world even when I didn't think the same about myself.

I needed to make a transition. My father told me, "Cammie, the number-one paying job without a degree is sales. You can sell anything to anybody if you believe in it." I got out of the restaurant business and started selling Canon color copiers, of all things. I know — random, right? And not just any copier; I'm talking about $60,000 to $70,000 machines. It was a big deal, and I sold the very first one in the southeast. I'll never forget my commission check. It was just ridiculous money for a girl from Bloomington.

One thing led to the next. David and I decided to start our own business. We called it Digital Connectivity. David was a techie, plus a talented computer graphic artist. We pitched to my dad and his business partner to help fund the company. We built a full-color service bureau, the first of its kind in the country, long before Kinkos. We grew to 30 employees and did trade shows all over the U.S. We were the Ken and Barbie of the digital world.

When you work with your spouse, dynamics change. I again was David's boss. It placed tremendous pressure on our marriage. Ours turned into a brother-sister relationship. The marriage didn't survive. Christopher was 13, Chase was six, and I was a single mother again at 34. I'm proud to say, to this day, David and I are great friends. In fact, he designed the cover for this book.

My time owning Digital Connectivity, and my participation in the emerging "tech" world enabled me to have a wonderful eight-year career at Hyperion Solutions. There, I led a powerful team who managed the relationships with our consulting partners (IBM, Deloitte, E.Y. and Accenture). The team will always have a very special place in my heart. I retired in 2007 as a senior vice president for Bank of America, ending my professional life with many accomplishments. I realize now that not having a degree did not hold me back. Do I wish I had finished? Yes. Am I proud of what I have accomplished without that piece of paper? Yes.

Christopher had grown into quite a young man. His identity, his character, his likes and dislikes had taken shape. He wanted to be a Navy SEAL. That was such a big deal to him. He knew he had what it took to become such a man. He and his best friend, Keith David, were both in Cub and Boy Scouts together, and the next thing they were going to do was become Seals. Everything was going as planned until he got to middle school.

There, he started being bullied, something he never shared with me until he was older. Christopher was extremely sensitive, just like his mother. He was a worrier. I never had to say anything about getting good grades. He was a perfectionist already, an overachiever even as a teenager. But he started holding all his stress in his gut. His stomach started hurting all day long.

Something didn't make sense. He started having diarrhea a couple of times a day, then five times a day, then 15, then 20. I took him to the doctor, and my journey took a sharp turn for the worse.

SCAN HERE FOR MORE

5

CIRCLING

For me, there are three types of anxiety: worrying about what might happen in the future, worrying about what is happening now, and worrying if what has happened before, will one day happen again. It was the night before I took Christopher to the doctor, and all three anxieties sat on my chest. I couldn't breathe. *But, it's just a doctor's visit*, I told myself. Children get sick. Children have stomach problems — but like most mothers, I imagined the worst.

I dozed off in that twilight space, where you're awake enough to hear what's going on in the house but exhausted enough to feel sleep quickly approaching. That's when I heard it, a faint melody. It was difficult to name the song, but the melody felt familiar. There was an echo, like being in an underground garage after leaving a concert early and the band was still playing. You can feel the energy, but the reverb makes it hard to understand the words. The closer I got to sleep, the closer the melody got to me. Then suddenly, I not only recognized the song, but I started singing along.

"Then sings my soul, my Savior God to Thee, How great Thou art, how great Thou art. Then sings my soul, my Savior God to Thee, How great Thou art, how great Thou art . . ."

That's odd. Bands don't play 'How Great Thou Art' in concert.

I reach to move my hair behind my right ear and notice I have on headphones. *Why are my headphones on in bed?* I think to myself. Then I feel someone in bed next to me. Frightened, I slowly open my eyes just enough to make out a nice woman waving as if to get my attention. She is smiling broadly, almost too broadly.

"Are you okay?" she asks in a soft, but deeply southern accent. "You've been asleep for a while," she adds.

I move my head slightly in front of her to see an oval-shaped window over her shoulder. Thick clouds are quickly passing in the background. I look up, "2-A" is written above my seat.

My God, I'm dreaming. I'm on that flight.

I rip my headphones off, jerk my body to the left and look behind me. The plane is packed. Everyone is here. The woman taps my shoulder causing me to reverse and face her again. She whispers secretly, "It's been an hour already."

"An hour?" I reply.

"Yes, we've been circling for an hour. We can't land."

"Why can't we land?" I ask.

"The pilot said we are headed toward peace, but there are unresolved issues and the tower won't give us clearance."

"And when I think that God, His Son not sparing" — the song is still audible through my headphones, which are now sitting on my lap still playing "How Great Thou Art." Frustrated, I reached quickly to press the off button. I ask the woman to explain what the pilot was talking about. She explains how everything was normal on the flight until about two hours ago. She says that's when we lost an engine and then temporarily lost power.

"The pilot did a phenomenal job getting back control of the aircraft," she details. "He had all the passengers from the back move toward the front and separate equally on both sides, as if we were waiting for someone to walk down the aisle. I knew something was wrong, though. I knew it because right before the pilot gave these instructions, the phone rang in that small kitchenette right up there." She points.

"When the attendant answered, I saw shock on her face. You know, you rarely see flight attendants get nervous, but the lady was nervous," she says. I try to get a word in, but can't find an entry point. She keeps talking.

"We need to land, but there is only one problem. The tower located in the city of Peace does not allow any passengers to bring baggage — literally or figuratively. Peace requires we let go of everything we got on board with. You see, I've traveled this leg before, many years ago, and the city of Peace would rather see us not make it before it allows people on the ground to be changed by unresolved issues coming from the sky. They protect their peace."

"These dreams are out of control," I'm thinking to myself. I was just about to take my son to the doctor. I'm not certain why I'm here, or what is going on. I reach for the bottled water in the pouch in front of me and splashed some on my face. I figured it would wake me up. It didn't. All it did was wet my face.

"Need a napkin?" the woman next to me offers.

"Yes, thank you."

This is no ordinary dream. Everything is real. The seats, the smell, the flight attendants and passengers — everything is just like it is in real life. My discomfort is increasing. My seat belt is so tight I can't freely move, so I unbuckle and reach up for the call button to request a flight attendant. That's when the plane drops altitude pushing me up and jamming my index finger. I let out a shriek that is covered by the gasps of other passengers surprised by the sudden drop. I am ejected out of my seat. I lay on my backside in the narrow aisle.

"All passengers return to their seats with your seat belts on. We are encountering some rough air," the pilot announces.

I place my hands behind me to get up when someone's hands slip underneath my armpits from behind.

"C'mon, I'll help you," a voice says. A stately man, standing about six-foot-three, lifts me up from behind and places me directly in my seat. He grabs my seat belt and fastens it tightly.

"Are you a flight attendant?" I ask. He has on a blue business suit, as if he may be a part of the crew. "I was trying to call a flight attendant when I fell. I think I broke my finger," I continue. The plane again shifts violently, shoving this man onto my lap. An older woman sitting across the aisle in 2-C leans forward and, with anger, shouts, "John, get back to your seat! You cannot help her yet."

This tall, kind man lifts himself off of me, kisses my forehead and walks all the way to the back of the airplane, touching the tops of each seat for balance. *Who was that?* I think. I have this strange feeling of connection, but panic doesn't allow time to ponder. Sliding food trays combined with the nervous moaning of passengers makes for a harmony of fright. The plane is convulsing as if we are flying on fumes. *Who is that man? Why did that lady speak to him that way? How does she know his name?* My mind is still reaching for answers.

The pilot again asks for our attention.

"Ladies and gentlemen, this is your captain speaking. We are about 150 miles away from Peace. We have a problem. The tower is still preventing us from landing due to one or more passengers on board. Heavenly Airlines transmits a list not only of our passengers, but of their hearts. We send ahead an entire summary of your life, your family and friends, your successes and your failures. The tower knows everything you have done, and everything you have not done. The tower knows everything you have said, and everything you have yet to say. Listen to me closely. If we are not able to land in Peace, I will have to detour and land 300 miles to the north, in Grudge."

Passengers are looking at each other in confusion. The woman next to me closes her eyes, smiles and hoods her head. She is the only one who knows what is coming next. The pilot continues

"The city of Grudge only takes incoming flights. Again, the city of Grudge only takes incoming flights. Once you land, you can never take off again. Right after a plane arrives in Grudge, it is destroyed, so leaving is never an option. We will be stuck in Grudge forever. We have one more chance to solve whatever issues must be solved on board before we run out of gas circling around the city of Peace. Flight attendants will be coming row by row to ask each person if there is anything we need to know, any confessions or any apologies. We can solve it right now, and the city of Peace will allow us to land. Flight attendants, please prepare the cabin for honesty. Please hear me," the pilot says in closing. "We only have one hour of fuel before we are going to have to put this plane down. If there is anything you need to say, please, I beg of you, say it now."

The plane is eerily quiet. No laughter, no crying, no nothing.

Each person begins to think about what needs to be made right and how to make it right now. No one wants to land in Grudge and be stuck forever. The flight attendants start walking to the rear of the plane to ask each person, one by one, whether there is anything that needs to be said, but, even before they can get to each row, I hear people voluntarily confess unresolved issues one to another.

The pilot's announcement triggers something in all of us. The very thought that we are so close to peace but will never get there because of something unresolved in our hearts causes us to speak up. Life, as we know it, is on the line. I hear a conversation behind me that sounds like a financial officer speaking to his boss.

"Bill, in 2008, when we couldn't find the $800,000 missing from our records — we couldn't find it because I took it. I stole the money. I was wrong, and I am asking right now for your forgiveness," the man says. "I am willing to make it up in any way I have to. I want to take full responsibility for my actions. Will you please forgive me?"

The boss, who is substantially older than his subordinate, looks disappointed but almost immediately responds, "I forgive you." In that instant, a green light comes on right above their seats. Then another conversation rings out.

"Sweetheart, I cheated, and I cheated for many years," another man confesses to his wife. "Those monthly trips to Kansas headquarters were not necessary for work. I was with another woman. If you want a divorce, I fully understand, and I have no excuses for what I've done to our family, the pain I've caused, and the violation of your trust. I will take whatever consequence I get."

His wife cries hysterically. Her shaking hands hover in front of her lips as her eyes scan for something that makes sense. After two minutes, she speaks the words that lit the green light above them: "I forgive you."

All of this is going on around me. One by one, the most transparent of conversations are happening.

My God, what is going on? I wonder.

Several minutes pass, and now I'm racking my brain to make sure there is nothing I need to say. The pilot comes back on the speaker.

"We can only circle for a few more minutes before we must head toward Grudge," he says in a matter-of-fact voice.

I turn around to see the progress of the confessions behind me. From the back row, where John is sitting, all the way to about five rows behind me, everything is green. People are holding each other tight. Children are confessing to parents, and parents to children. One conversation really touches me. A wife expresses regret to her husband for the way she acted before his mother passed. In tears, she apologizes for not welcoming his mother into their home in the years before she died. She asks him to forgive her for encouraging him to place his mother in a nursing home. It is a most gut-wrenching dialogue in the midst of the most pressure-filled emergency situation you will ever dream of. Right now, I notice something. I notice peace.

The conversations, even during a time of emergency, start to bring calm onto the plane. Right when we are trying to land in Peace, peace begins to land in us. Everyone's countenance is changing. We are making everything right with those we care about. No matter where we end up, if we have unresolved issues, we will not truly be at peace. I am starting to get it. The woman next to me taps my shoulder again.

"While you were sleeping, I was a bit jealous," she says. "I looked at your shoes, your purse, your hair and your nails. I had negative thoughts about you because you are so pretty, and me? Not so much. I want to say I'm sorry for thinking negative thoughts about you and ask for your forgiveness."

I don't know how to respond. It is odd, but I appreciate her honesty.

"Of course, I forgive you." But even after my words, no green light comes on.

The pilot makes one last announcement. "Has everyone made everything right? If not, we are going to have to detour. We do not have clearance."

The flight attendant is one row behind me, now. Confessions are getting faster and more to the point. The entire plane is green at every row, with the exception of two, mine and the row behind me. That's where Ted is sitting.

"Sir, is there anything?" the flight attendant asks. She repeats herself in shorthand.

"Sir?" Ted looks directly at me.

"Cammie, I'm sorry." Instantly, the green light above his row comes on.

"This is our last chance," the pilot announces, this time with a tinge of something in his voice that wasn't there before. My row is the last row. The entire plane is looking directly at me. The flight attendant is standing over me. I am speechless. "How do I clear my heart? What am I not remembering?"

The plane makes a hard left bank. We are changing directions. Passengers are looking at me with tears in their eyes. Their fists gesture in front of their chests as if to say, "Please remember, for the sake of us all." I close my eyes.

"Oh, God, please show me what is in my heart that I cannot see."

"We cannot circle any longer," the pilot says. "Who is holding something back?"

The flight attendant drops to one knee, presses her sweating palms into mine and asks the question, "Is it you?"

SCAN HERE FOR MORE

6

THE HELL
BENEATH HELL

"I s it you?" the flight attendant asks again, but her voice sounds different this time. "Ma'am?" she presses.

I feel someone touching my shoulder and turn to see if it is the same woman sitting next to me.

"Mom? Do you hear the lady talking to you? She's asking you a question."

I blinked, and my son Christopher was standing next to me. The room was pale, with faded orange and gray horizontal lines on the walls. An office assistant in blue scrubs was standing in front of me with a pen in one hand and a copy of my insurance card in the other. We stared at each other in a kind of stalemate. She calmly and with concern asked again, "Cammie, who is the primary person on your health insurance? Is it you?"

I didn't know how long she had been standing there asking this question, but the entire waiting room was waiting for me to answer. Even the pretty little girl in the middle of the floor in the children's play area stopped the red train from moving down its plastic track; she was waiting too. I zoned back in and answered.

"It's me, yes. I am the primary." Christopher, with his hand still on my shoulder, expressed concern.

"Are you all right, Mom?"

"Yes," I answered. "I was just daydreaming, I guess. I'm good."

We sat down and waited to be called back into the doctor's office. We needed to get to the bottom of Christopher's pain and discomfort. He was a school-aged kid, too young to go through what he was going through. It was a time to play, make great friends, try your hand at sports, and in every way enjoy a normal life, but after that day, nothing would ever be normal again.

After multiple tests, Christopher was diagnosed with ulcerative colitis (UC).

"Ulcerative what?" I asked the doctor. I'd never heard of it and knew nothing about the seriousness of the disease. The learning curve was a steep one, but I started to climb. I first learned that UC develops over time, which makes it hard to see it coming. It's a bowel disease with no known cure. It causes inflammation and painful sores in the digestive tract, affecting the deepest lining of the colon and rectum. It is painful to witness, more horrific to experience. Basically, UC is a messy and all-around debilitating condition. That day in the doctor's office, and in the years to follow, I scrambled to get my hands on everything available to know about this condition. When your child's life is on the line, you become a quick study.

I learned UC is a cousin of Crohn's disease and microscopic colitis. It's more common among men in the western world than anywhere else, which leads many to believe it's a result of a particularly American lifestyle and diet. Some of the better-known theories involve a dysfunctional immune system, environmental factors, changes in an individual's gut bacteria and even genetics.

I remember sitting in the doctor's office and going over a laundry list of Christopher's symptoms. It's hard to write about, but this journey was teaching me that people going through hell need to hear from someone who has been there and back. My son's diarrhea had gotten worse. It was now bloody and filled with pus. He had excruciating abdominal pain, rectal pain, rectal bleeding, urgency or inability to defecate, fatigue, fever and weight loss. In other words, hell.

From the day of his diagnosis, and for the next three years, we had what felt like hundreds of doctor visits, but one visit stood out above them all. On that day, his doctor looked at us both and said, "If you don't get this out, he's going to get colon cancer," pointing to an X-ray of Christopher's colon.

A mother never forgets such a sentence, such a picture, such a feeling. My heart sank. It felt like my tears were on fire. "Cancer?" *What was this doctor talking about?* This was so out of the blue. "Cancer?" I couldn't believe my ears. Christopher's physician was adamant: something needed to be done quickly.

"We must move now," he said. "Time is of the essence."

Now just go with me here. All of this took place during the Christmas season. They wanted to remove his colon right away so he could take the holidays to recover. He was a young man, already accustomed to internalizing his angst and overthinking, and the need for major, organ-removing surgery set his anxiety into overdrive. He panicked, and so did I. If you are a parent, then you know there is someone so loved that words can never convey just how much. That someone is *our child.*

It can be nearly impossible to be happy or content when your child is suffering. How do you smile, laugh or even enjoy a meal? How do you make vacation plans, go out with friends or even sit down and watch mindless television when your child is in hell? It is almost as if being happy is offensive when your child is not, and therein lies one of the greatest, dare I say, diabolical challenges on this journey: the challenge to be at peace in the midst of war, or, in my case, the challenge of keeping your cool when your life has become a fiery furnace.

Doctors wanted my son's colon out immediately. They stressed the importance of having a positive mindset prior to major surgery, but Christopher was terrified. His mind was not in the right place. He hated what the operation meant to him physically. He felt he would somehow end up freakish. He was uncomfortable with the doctor's declaration that he needed the operation so urgently. The immediacy caused stress, which only worsened his current condition, and the worsened condition then caused him greater stress. A vicious cycle began.

In retrospect, I should've postponed the colon removal surgery at that point. Christopher was so ill-prepared for it, but I kept remembering, in horror, the words the doctor had said, "If you don't get this surgery now, he's going to get cancer." So, we pushed forward. It had to be done, we were told. Remove the colon, spend 60 days recuperating, and Christopher will be recovered by springtime. They made it sound routine. It was just the opposite.

Christopher's surgery took several hours. Technically, the surgery was a success. The operating team removed his colon. But, in the process, they punctured his small intestine. Yes, when they were removing his colon, they severely punctured his bowel. Right when we thought things would get better, they got worse. *One* major internal organ issue had suddenly become *two*.

Christopher was devastated. I was numb. It was a nightmare, something I'd never imagined was even possible. Recovery became a heavier burden. Oh my God, there was more.

I was sitting right there, in the hospital room, one day. Christopher was having a PICC line inserted when the medical professional punctured his lung. You read that correctly. She *punctured* his lung. If I weren't there, I would believe this was a made-up melodrama. It was unbelievable. As soon as it happened, Christopher was struggling to breathe. *Two* major internal organ issues suddenly became *three*. It was an unmitigated fiasco. Christopher's hospital stay expanded to three solid months. His mental disposition, which wasn't overly optimistic to begin with, deteriorated significantly with each passing moment. He would lay in bed and cry, or just sleep for hours on end. To see my son so utterly devastated was dreadful. At this point, the hospital really should have conducted a psychiatric evaluation — he was in so much physical pain, so much mental anguish. Depression set in. He had a morphine drip that discharged with the push of a button. Christopher would press it feverishly and continually, like a troubled *Jeopardy* contestant, a child experiencing the suffering of an adult.

One weekend, while in the hospital, his normal doctor was not on call. A substitute physician was filling in. I'll never forget it. The doctor entered the room and out of nowhere began verbally abusing Christopher.

"You need to get out of this bed," the doctor practically screamed. "If you don't get out of this bed, more things are going to go bad for you!" He spoke as if Christopher had punctured his own bowel and lung. I sat there so shocked, it took a couple of seconds to digest. This doctor continued to barrage my son with more negativity. His bedside manner was non-existent. He continued berating about the need to *move*, about the threat of *more bad things* happening. I'd had enough. I grabbed the doctor's white lab coat. He turned from Christopher to me, surprised someone would put their hands on him. In my mind, he had started the foolishness, and I was going to finish it.

"*Excuse* me," I said. "We need to talk outside. *Now!*"

I turned into the exorcist. I walked out of the hospital room and dared him not to follow. I could hear the physician's footsteps trailing behind me.

In the hallway, I closed the door to Christopher's room and turned to the doctor, face to face. I was livid, seething. It was time to rip him a new one. "Who do you think you are?" I asked. It was rhetorical. I needed no response. "My son is ready to give up, and you're talking to him like that?" I yelled loud enough to turn a few heads of nearby nurses. "Do not come back to see my son — ever again. Do you understand me? Leave!" I screamed.

He left. That felt good. Until that point, it was like we were just punching bags being boxed around by whoever wanted to hit us. It was time to hit back. We would be respected. We would be treated with decency. My son would not be prodded. It was time to stop crying and feeling bad for ourselves.

It was time to fight.

I walked to the nurses' station and asked for that doctor never to see my son again. I tracked down my son's primary surgeon and requested the exact same thing. More surgeries were to come, and the next one — you guessed it — would make things even worse. Now that there was no colon, a punctured bowel, and a punctured lung, our concerns about him having diarrhea turned to whether he would ever be able to have a bowel movement at all. Our conversations, which were already serious, went to another level. My son had a quarter-size hole in his side. I could see into his stomach. The J-pouch surgery which we were about to get, would cover up this hole.

"Let me explain something to you, Mom. If this J-pouch

didn't exist, I would commit suicide." His words left me speechless. Christopher meant what he said. I could tell he intended
to move forward with the threat. "There is *no way* I will live
with this bag. You can *forget* that. It's *not* going to happen. We're
either going to get this J-pouch or I *will* commit suicide."

No teenage boy wants to wear a poop bag, especially a teenage boy. How would he date? How would he hug girls? Would
they smell it? Would they ever touch him? The *thought* alone was
humiliating.

It made noise. It covered a hole that led directly into his
stomach. It was unsightly and irritated the skin to which it was
attached. It interfered with any attempt at intimacy or physical
activity. It could sometimes be quite odorous. Several times a
day, I had to help him drain the bag and change it and make sure
everything was sterile. We were in the hell that's beneath hell.

In the end, we got rid of the old bag, replacing it with the
J-pouch instead. The J-pouch procedure removes the damaged
tissue of the colon and allows the patient to continue having rel-
atively normal bowel movements, meaning stool leaves the body
through the anus. But all bowel movements are *now*, as in, pull
over immediately or you'll have an accident. It was an upgrade,
but it also had its risks.

Aside from the usual surgical concerns such as reaction
to anesthesia or complications like blood clots, pneumonia, or
sepsis, the J-pouch procedure may cause internal or external
bleeding. There may be complications where muscular movements of the intestines cease. Any narrowing of the digestive
tract would prevent the movement of food and stools. These
were enough risks to terrify any mother. It may be months after
the surgery before a patient reaches a new normal in terms of
bowel movements — which are never really "normal" by typical

standards. Even then, it's often messy, usually five or six move-ments each day, having the consistency of mashed potatoes. For any young man, such a forced adaptation makes for an alarming and difficult adjustment. Christopher was no different.

We had the operation. I never forgot his warning about what would happen if we didn't.

It was after the operation, after the J-Pouch took its place in his body, that the bullying began. At Collins Hill High School in Georgia, Christopher wasn't a jock, which was a prerequisite to hang with the popular crowd. So, he kept to himself. He read a lot of books; he dreamed of going to MIT and becoming a Navy Seal. Somewhere along the way, he began to escape his reality by smoking pot with the stoners. He played a lot of video games, got into a little trouble once or twice, but never anything major.

Next to Keith, the one constant positive element in Christopher's life was Emily. She became his girlfriend in high school and was there for over 10 years. Emily eventually left to study at Augusta University, and Christopher followed her there. He said he always wanted an Ivy League education, but he stayed in Georgia. Emily was Catholic, so Christopher began studying Catholicism. He received all the sacraments and com-pleted the entire confirmation process. I watched him proudly receive his First Communion from his new parish priest, and he became an active member of the local Knights of Columbus. Later, Christopher and Emily would expand their religious hori-zons and study Buddhism together.

At first, Christopher and Emily were friends; then they became engaged; then they broke off the engagement and became friends again. Emily understood his medical issues and loved him unconditionally. Emily was well-versed in the language of UC. She had learned her way around a J-pouch. She could swap out a bowel movement for a fresh, clean bag in no time flat. She loved him, but being his caretaker wasn't what Christopher wanted for Emily. He began to see her differently, as if he were a patient and she, was his nurse. This placed them on different paths. Slowly, they grew apart.

"No other woman is ever going to accept this," Christopher would say to me. "I'm never going to be able to get another woman, Mom. Ever."

I wish things were different, but they were not. I wish my son never had this terrible disease, but he did. God allowed this trial into our lives. We don't control the roller coaster. It is our job to simply hold on.

Innovation in medicine has taught us so much more about UC than was available just a few years ago. For most patients, finding the right foods is key. Dietary changes, such as adopting a high-calorie or lactose-free diet, may improve symptoms. In Christopher's case, we were told very little about the importance of diet. Looking back, it makes so much sense. The colon is where the food is; why weren't we concentrating on the food? There are also several medications today that treat symptoms and bring about remission in patients; including mesalamine, sulfasalazine, steroids and immunosuppressants. All of this may help to decrease diarrhea and increase bowel control. There's still no cure, but treatment can greatly improve a patient's quality of life. With appropriate treatment, life expectancy is the same as that of the general population.

At the age of seventeen, after a major surgery, Christopher left the hospital more wounded than when he arrived. He was admitted with a colon issue. By the end of his stay, there were holes in Christopher's body and spirit. The surgery was a disaster. This made for a rocky life ahead. To help with the pain, his doctor gave him 90 OxyContin pills with a prescription for more.

SCAN HERE FOR MORE

7

GROOMED FOR ADDICTION

octors are sources of skill and wisdom. Attempt to criticize their practices, and your words may go unheard. The sheer reverence our society has for professionals who wear the long white coat is remarkable. This reverence is felt because doctors are often the last line of defense between life and death. Even the leader of the free world must follow a doctor's orders.

We walked out of that hospital with 90 OxyContin pills. I remember the bottle. It was a tall, smoky, orange-colored cylinder. The instructions were to take one pill every four hours for pain. I made sure that happened. I didn't know any better. It is difficult to describe the pain these pain killers caused. What was meant for good, was pure evil. What was meant to allow healing, instead opened a wound that would never be healed — a psychological wound, a chemical wound much greater than the punctures in my son's lung and bowel. There is medicine to stop physical bleeding; there is surgery to close a gaping hole in the physical body; but what do you do when your thoughts begin to bleed? What do you do when your very being is hemorrhaging? From the moment we left the hospital, Christopher was dying more than he was living.

His treatment became his sickness. His cure became his problem. Ask anyone who suffers from opioid abuse, and they'll tell you, no one intends to become addicted. They intend to get rid of the pain — the pain of an injury, the pain from surgery. In many ways, I am touching the forbidden third rail here, and I must be careful to say precisely what I mean. I have a love-hate relationship with doctors. We need them. We cannot live without those who skillfully care for the diseased, the hurt and the wounded. But, some of the medicines prescribed are often more dangerous than the sicknesses they are intended to heal.

Christopher started taking the pills, and soon the pills began taking him. Our mother-son relationship transformed nearly overnight. Someone who had been a kind, loving and considerate young man morphed into someone who, at times, I did not recognize.

Every day, he took opioids. Every single day. I was in charge of keeping track of the time between pills, and, if there was ever a moment when I wasn't on time with the next dose, things got testy. He was only 17, and a senior in high school at Collins Hill. He wasn't prepared to bear the weight of such a powerful narcotic.

I was a single mother, trying to keep a roof over our heads, while caring for a terribly sick child. Things were sliding toward hell. I remember sitting on the edge of my bed listening to Christopher moan in pain in the next room. His body had been prodded and poked more than many people three times his age. I began to wonder whether there was anything I could have done differently.

There was: I should never have allowed his doctor to rob my son of pivotal moments that would never happen again. His doctor rushed us into surgery right before graduation, causing Christopher to miss walking with his class. As a result, he earned a GED instead of a traditional diploma, although he was an AP student.

This was a blow to his ego.

His sickness caused him to miss his prom. As he approached his 18th birthday, I could tell he was as wounded in his spirit as he was in his body. The light in his eyes slowly dimmed, and it tore me to pieces. Little did I know that was just the beginning. Heading our way was a greater challenge than I could have ever imagined.

Before the doctor sent us home with those pills on that fateful day, I wish he would have taken a moment, pulled us aside, and just said, "Here's the name of a therapist. You and Christopher need to book a session right away." This kind of advice could have changed everything. We should have been prepared mentally for what we both were about to encounter. His body was ravaged. Why didn't they tell us he would be managing pain for a long time? There was a storm forming, and no one said a word. I was in my late 30s, and I'd never seen a therapist or counselor before. I didn't know what I didn't know. There was no one in the hospital whose job it was to educate us on our medicine. The system was too occupied with addressing the fifth vital sign, pain. No one said a word about the dangers of OxyContin. If I didn't know better, I would say Christopher was being groomed for addiction.

Think about it. In the hospital, he had a morphine drip. Just press a button and feel good. The pain goes away instantly. How does this affect a teenage boy? After 70 days in the hospital, the drip became a watering hole. He pressed the button all day long. The reality was, he had an issue before we even checked out. He was groomed.

I have to say one more thing. We were never given an alternative to OxyContin. I was never told to give him Motrin or Tylenol or ice for pain. Nothing but OxyContin. There were never any restrictions or guidelines either — just take the pill, take another one, and then take one more. If I had to do it all over again, if God gave me one more chance, I would go on a mission to find holistic answers to address his condition.

I did pay close attention to his food. For example, I knew he couldn't have popcorn. I knew lettuce bothered him because that was a hard thing to digest. If I knew what I know today, I would have looked far and wide for natural, dietary remedies from the day he was diagnosed with ulcerative colitis as a young boy. The part of his body that was diseased was the part that processed his food. It seems so obvious now, but I never thought about looking for foods that healed the body. I should have exhausted all other options before allowing them to operate on my son.

If I had another chance — please hear me — we both would go to a therapist together and separately, but that never happened. Life took a different turn, and, over the next few years, Christopher, my son, became an addict.

We needed help. It hurts me to even write those words, but I have to. My son became a drug addict. Why didn't I do more? We needed help. He needed help. I wish someone would have helped us.

I'm writing this to help somebody. I don't know who you are, but be careful when you are being rushed to make critical medical decisions. My doctor friends tell me there are often situations where you don't have time to wait, and I fully understand that. But it just seemed our surgeons wanted to prescribe, rinse and repeat. Nobody wanted to take a moment and think about Christopher's future. He was just a kid.

Once, we were a good distance from where we lived in Atlanta, and Christopher became ill. Now, this was after his J-pouch operation. There was no time to get back to the city, so I took him to a nearby hospital in Gwinnett County, which is north of downtown Atlanta.

After the ER doctor examined him, he came directly to me and said, "It's very serious. He has a blockage. We have to go into surgery immediately."

"Well, our doctors are at St. Joseph's," I said. That seemed to annoy him. We stood in the hallway, and I went ahead and asked, "How many surgeries have you done like this before?"

He looked at me and said, "Enough — and you don't have a choice. I'm the only one here, and I have to operate on him now." His attitude was, "Lady, I don't have time to let you evaluate me. I have to go to surgery right this second." Everything was always an emergency. Always.

Back into surgery we went. They found a blockage in his small intestines. They couldn't get it to move through so they had to cut one end of his already damaged intestines, cut the other end, remove the blocked area in between, and then sew the remaining intestines back together. Guess what happened next? They put him back on opioids. We were in a vicious cycle. From that point forward, any time Christopher had gas or discomfort in his abdomen, he immediately thought he had another blockage. We took countless trips to the ER for what turned out to be indigestion.

We saw no end in sight. Our home looked like a research lab, with empty pill bottles everywhere. Then, one day, I decided to look deeper into how and why opioids are allowed to destroy lives. What I found made me question whether it was wise for me to have gone looking in the first place. The facts aren't especially interesting, but it is necessary to go through them to truly appreciate the problem.

This was the early 2000s, pharmaceutical companies promised the American medical community that patients treated with opioid pain relievers would not become addicted. Their statements sounded simple enough. These companies assured doctors and health leaders everywhere that opioids, the pharmaceutical concoctions now known to be among the world's most addictive substances, were not something to be feared. Big Pharma made it easy. Doctors made it profitable. More on this later.

Over the past 20 years, more than 500,000 people have died from opioid overdoses. The statistics don't tell the story of a son, daughter, neighbor, or friend. By the time Christopher was in his mid-20s, he was so beaten up, so over-prescribed, and so depressed that he was ready — he was ready to go.

"Please, Mom, my body is frail. Please, just let me go," he would say. "Let me die. I can't take this anymore. I don't have the strength." I would make him stop talking like that, but it scared me to my core. "Mom, I'm going to go before you. I want you to be ready." I would not let my boy give up, and, while we persisted, more challenges came our way. I wish I could say we got control of his addiction. I wish I could say he is still healing. I can say neither because what was waiting for us — not only in Atlanta but also in Hong Kong, and, ultimately, Cambodia — is so unreal that, if I had I not been there to witness the events myself, no one would ever convince me the story is true.

SCAN HERE FOR MORE

8

LIGHT IN THE DARK

The good thing about hell is, it doesn't last forever. No matter how violent the storm, the sun will eventually shine again. Christopher and I were in a storm. He was managing his sickness, I was managing him, and we both were managing our emotions. We were exhausted. On top of that, bills and the other basic necessities of life still had to be taken care of. It was a recipe for burnout. It was also a recipe for listening.

My ears, my heart and my spirit were open. What I mean is, I could no longer do everything alone. Having a sick child will humble you in the blink of an eye. You learn your strengths, your weaknesses, your capacity, and your limits. The random nature of his illness discouraged me from physically being away from Christopher for long periods of time, but I needed a better job, and the interview for the job I was seeking was in Canada — Vancouver, to be exact. I wouldn't be gone long. Just fly up, interview, and get right back to Atlanta — at least, that was the plan.

After the interview, I went back to my hotel and sat on the edge of the bed. It was quiet, too quiet. That's when I received a call. In the state I was in, phone calls were a horrific sound. I didn't want to look at the caller ID. Was it a hospital, a doctor, or my son? For a moment, I froze watching the phone ring face down on my bed. Slowly reaching for it, I turned the phone over. It was my best friend, Genevieve. *Why would she be calling?* I thought to myself. I moved to the edge of the bed and answered.

"Hello?"

She cut to the chase. "I have the perfect man for you."

It's just like a best friend to call with the most random statement. "I'm well; how are you, friend?" I responded.

"Oh, hey, Cammie. I'm good. Got somebody for you to meet." I could hear the smile in her voice.

"Of course, *you* have," I answered sarcastically. "You've never liked *anyone* I dated. There's always something wrong with them. Always something." I sighed. "Even that one time when — "

"Not with this guy," Genevieve interrupted. There was a brief pause on the phone. I could tell my friend meant business about her new find; she had given this one some thought. "I'm setting you up on a date."

In my mind, there was only one problem: I hated blind dates. "Let me get this straight. *You're* going to pick out a guy for me because I do such a poor job of picking for *myself?*" I asked, half-amused.

"Yep."

"Really?"

"Yep."

"Fine," I said. "If you wanna fix me up with somebody, *fine.*"

Genevieve went on to explain. She had gotten to know him when a magazine she was working for presented him with an award. She'd been playing Cupid behind the scenes for a while before approaching either of us.

"Listen, Cammie, if you don't '*like* him, like him,' you're still going to like him as a friend," she said. "You'll make a new friend if nothing else. You've got nothing to lose, really, but I think . . ." My friend was making very interesting statements. When I thought about it, though, she was hedging. She was really saying, "either you'll have a friend or a husband." The two are pretty far apart, but I played along.

"What's his name?" I blurted out.

"John," Genevieve said.

"Okay, John *who*, Genevieve?"

"I'm not going to tell you his last name. I don't want you Googling him."

"That's not fair," I responded. "I'm in Vancouver at a job interview, and my patience is growing thin. I love you, but maybe we should speak when I get back to the United States."

"It's better this way, trust me," Genevieve said. "I think you're going to like him, Cammie, really, I do. But remember: if not, you can always be friends."

A blind date was arranged. In April 2006, I walked into the Bluepointe restaurant in the Buckhead district of Atlanta to meet my best friend's selection. It seemed we were looking for each other because our eyes met at nearly the same time.

"Are you Cammie?" A tall, stately, soft-spoken man inquired.

"Yes, are you John?"

"I am." We smiled and hugged like we knew each other from another life. It was comfortable.

"She was right!" I said to myself without letting John know excitement was brewing underneath. He was a gentleman, with no fake conversation, no filler, just dialogue about real life. As the conversation went on, we got into our professional lives. He said he worked for General Electric and that he managed a few people. His job kept him on the road a lot, or, more correctly, in the air. John said he usually woke up at 4:30 a.m. on weekdays to work out before starting his day. He would then jump on a flight to another country and continued with meetings until late.

He seemed attentive and disciplined and unbelievably busy but fully and comfortably in control of his life and surroundings. He wasn't boastful in any way or full of himself. I've met those men before. He was quite the opposite. John asked about my life and seemed genuinely interested when I talked about what was going on with me. It was good to have a listening ear. I didn't even know how badly I needed one.

We shared sushi and sashimi off the same plate, in a pre-Covid kind of way, and flowed from subject to subject without awkward transitions. We laughed easily and often. It was like we'd known each other forever. By the end of the evening, we had agreed to go out again, which we did, and, after that, it was onto a third date.

On our third date, I led with the news that I'd received a tremendous job offer from Bank of America. The first night we met, I let him know I had just returned from an interview in Canada, so he knew I was on the job market. If I took the Bank of America job, I would need to move to Charlotte, North Carolina. The second I mentioned Charlotte, John's face fell. I didn't know how to feel.

"I would have never asked you out if Genevieve had told me you were going to live outside Atlanta," he said. His words stabbed the air. The air started to bleed. "I mean — well, it's complicated," he said. I just sat there looking at him. He continued explaining. "I travel a lot, so my ex-wife is at the house during the week with the boys. I mean, I'm going to stay here in Atlanta at least until they get out of high school. You and I both live here, so I thought . . ."

"Well, the money for the Charlotte job is great. I'm a single mom," I said.

"If things are meant to be — you know, between us and all — then they're meant to be."

John said he understood, never breaking his calm demeanor.

He went on to provide wise counsel as I moved to North Carolina and into management at Bank of America. A few weeks later, he helped me get moved into my Carolina condominium and took the time to hang my pictures on the wall — which was something I really liked for some reason.

This was the first time I had lived alone, with no boyfriend, husband, or kids in the house. Christopher was in college in Augusta with his girlfriend. I was uneasy but confident she could handle anything that came up, and I could get to him within a few hours. John and I saw each other on the weekends. The career move was professionally rewarding and, to my surprise, my relationship with John grew.

At some point, the subject of marriage came up. I don't recall who said it first or in what context, but the atmosphere got serious really quickly. I'd done the marriage thing before, and the next time — if there *was* to be a next time — would be my last. I was certain of that.

"If I ever get married again," I told John, "*that* will be the name on my tombstone." Marriage and tombstone talk ramped the stakes up pretty quickly. We got on the fast track. Genevieve was right. John was the one.

Ours was a Cinderella story. That's the best way to describe my romance with Mr. John Rice. Yes, I knew his last name. I never really knew what *right* felt like until I met him. I had failed relationships in my past, so had he. We both needed mulligans. I'd gotten pregnant with Christopher and quickly married Ted too young. My time with Ted was a high school love extended too long.

This, however, was on a different level. We seemed to complement each other in ways I didn't know a couple could. I met John when I was 45 years old. In my four-and-a-half decades prior to our Bluepointe sushi dinner blind date, I had not experienced anything like what his presence made me feel. He was reliable. He was strong in every aspect. The most integrity of anyone I had known. It took a while to restore my trust in a partner, but John restored it completely.

John had a nearly pastoral demeanor. He was calm. He was reassuring. He was one of the greatest businessmen on earth but didn't walk around trying to impress others. He didn't have to make people feel small for him to feel big. Instead, John was encouraging, supportive, thoughtful, and kind. To have these traits, and still be successful in business, is rare. He was rare. Genevieve was right!

In our early dating days, I remember being introduced to John's office assistant, Judy, and noting how busy he was. Judy gave me a copy of his calendar, with daily meetings and commitments booked solid for an entire year. On the few open days each month, Judy and I scheduled dates, which often required plane reservations, too. This was a different type of Cinderella story, a jet-setting one. John led his employees by comfort, not by command. If he said it, he would do it. That was huge, especially for a woman. I had never heard him make an excuse, and he does not lie, ever. Trust me, I've checked for it, even for little embellishments here and there. Genevieve was right again!

During our first year dating, I recorded everything we did. I read my journal again recently and, truly, it seems like a fairy tale. Every date, every trip, every conversation between us is jotted down somewhere in the book. There's a journal entry on our first General Electric Christmas party. John is a former vice chairman of General Electric, by the way. The party was a big deal because he hadn't brought a date since his divorce years earlier. When you're on the arm of one of Atlanta's most eligible bachelors, you get put under a microscope rather suddenly. I wrote about feeling the eyes of his colleagues staring right through me. I journaled about the litany of questions I received during small talk, as people calculated my potential as a suitable companion for Mr. Rice. "Where do you work? How many kids do you have? Where are you from originally?" I felt like a first lady or something.

The reason why Genevieve recommended me started to make sense. I'm a chameleon in that I could wear whatever hat was required, play whatever role was needed. In fact, one of the marketing lines she gave John initially when trying to convince him to go on the blind date was that he could take me from the BBQ to the boardroom. She was right. Whether it was sitting at dinner next to a prime minister, chatting up one of GE's top clients, or talking with the locals on a tour of an orphanage, I adapted. I learned very early on that being with John meant positively impacting lives. What a beautiful, honorable mandate.

Oh, and about his family: John's family welcomed me warmly into their lives, which I so greatly appreciated. They were *Leave It to Beaver* in the flesh, so wonderfully normal, and they truly enjoyed each other's company. They reminded me of growing up in Bloomington — the family reunions and Fourth of July cookouts, all were so warm. I found myself loving his family as my own. Many corporate bigwigs are self-centered. They believe the sun comes out in the morning especially to shine on them. After meeting John's family, I understood why he was not that way: they, his parents, in particular, centered him. They always have. He was reared in a stable, loving, Christian environment and was taught responsibility from a young age. He landed a job with GE right out of college and displayed the hard work and dedication instilled in him by his mom and dad.

At GE, Jack Welch himself took a personal interest in John, mentoring and grooming him for increasingly significant positions and responsibilities. Jack particularly liked how John handled himself among his fellow employees, whether he was chatting up a VP in the office suite or a janitor on the shop floor. In an age when many CEOs are seemingly so much the same, concerned only with bottom lines and their own stock options, John was noticeably different.

On November 24, 2007, John and I were married. Genevieve gave us the best gift ever — each other! You should see the wedding video. Christopher gave a beautiful toast, the best ever. He worried about me a lot. We became so connected through struggle. I think he was just so happy I had John. Christopher saw in John a real, mature, solid man, and he didn't have a good opinion of men, so that was saying a lot. There was a bittersweetness to my marriage too. Christopher, through watching how John treated me, saw what he missed in a father in his own life. John had two sons from his first marriage, Steve and Tanner. My son would watch their interactions. You could almost see the longing in his eyes for what could have been if his biological father was as loving and present.

After the wedding, we started taking the boys skiing. Ironically, Chase, Steve and Christopher's birthdays are all in the same week, September 11, 17, and 18, respectively. It was the first time for Christopher and Chase; when I was a single mom, skiing didn't rank high on the list of priorities. On the other hand, Tanner and Steve have skied since they were three years old. So, we went on this ski trip somewhere near Paris. Now, when Christopher would get excited, he would eat too much, including a lot of exotic foods. We really had to keep an eye on him. I was skiing, I was watching and I was worried. We had a great time, though, and at last, it was time to fly home in time for Christmas Eve. We were racing through the Paris airport because we thought we were going to miss our connecting flight, and, if we did, we would be stuck in Paris on Christmas day.

We ran like rabbits through the airport trying to reach our flight. John and I were slower than the boys, so we had made a plan. Steve and Chase were supposed to run ahead and ask the people at the gate to hold the plane for us. However, they got on the plane, put their headphones on, and didn't say squat to anybody. So, John and I made it to the plane. Thank God for Tanner because he got them to hold the plane. We were in first class, and the boys were in the back. After about an hour, the flight attendants started feeding the passengers dinner. I went back to check on Christopher.

"Mom, I'm just not really feeling very good," he said.

"Okay, well, just drink some water, and I'll come back and check on you in a bit," I told him. I went back up front, had my wine, and ate some food. Then I laid back and placed my blanket up over my eyes.

"Ladies and gentlemen, is there a doctor on board?" I suddenly heard the pilot say loudly over the intercom. He said it again. "Is there a doctor on board?"

I jumped up like bloody murder. The guy sitting across the aisle from me jumped up, too. He looked directly at me.

"Are you a doctor?" he asked.

"No," I replied, "but I know it's my son. He's in trouble."

"I'm a doctor," he said.

"Come on, then." I grabbed his hand and rushed to the back of the plane. Christopher was on the bathroom floor. We opened the door enough to pick him up. He was sweating profusely and had thrown up. He burned with fever and was getting sicker by the second.

The flight attendants offered to help. "There's a space up in first class. Let's move him up there."

We moved him to first class and laid him flat. The doctor's nurse was on board too, and she came over. The doctor was checking Christopher's vitals. He was not doing well. The doctor was able to get an IV running and hung it right above the seat. The copilot stepped out of the cockpit and spoke to us.

"Look, the pilot says we need to know in the next 45 minutes if we have to make an emergency landing or not because, otherwise, we're going to be over water and won't be able to land."

The doctor thought for a second and responded. "I need more time. I need 30 minutes."

"Okay, doctor, what is your name?" the copilot asked.

"Dr. Rudolph. My name is Dr. Rudolph."

This is Christmas Eve, and that's his name? "You're lying," I said. "There is no way."

He looked back at me and said it again, "My name is Dr. Rudolph."

So, Dr. Rudolph was closely monitoring Christopher on Christmas Eve, giving him something for nausea. Our major concern was another intestinal blockage. If he had a blockage, we would have to land the plane. I was freaking out. It was excruciating. I rubbed his temples, rubbed the back of his neck, laid washcloths across his forehead, and held his hand. "You're going to be okay, son," I prayed over him.

After a few minutes, the doctor made his decision. "I think we've got it under control," he said.

I didn't sleep one second on that flight. We went on to our destination and landed in Atlanta, and the pilot announced, "Everybody, please stay seated." Because we had come in from Europe, they had to have somebody get on the plane to check our passports. They checked mine and John's and got us off the plane with Christopher as quickly as possible. An ambulance drove up to the plane and took us to the hospital.

"I don't think it's a blockage," I said to the ambulance driver after I climbed into the front seat. The ambulance driver, a young guy, looked at me and said, "So, tell me about your husband."

I burst out laughing. "You just made my day," I told him. "That's my son."

SCAN HERE FOR MORE

9

THE INVASION

hen I was a little girl, my mother taught me a secret. "If you're scared, if you're afraid, close your eyes, Cammie," she would say. "Surround yourself with white light." At the time, I had no idea if the advice was true. I didn't know if it would work, that is, until the night I felt the cold metal tip of a shotgun on my forehead. But, let me not get ahead of myself.

My mother was introducing me to manifestation. The ability to make the invisible become real. Manifestation brings your future into your now. Over the years, I discovered I had the gift. I could manifest. If I said something, if I set my heart and my mind on something, it would appear. We all have the power to call things into existence, but few of us use it. Words are power, and my words, my thoughts, and my intentions have changed my life.

It was 2009, John and I lived right outside of Atlanta in a suburb called Roswell. We were in a home a woman would die for — and I almost did. Like so many things in life, one moment, one decision, or in my case, one T-shirt can change everything.

I'll explain. Long after that Christmas evening plane ride from hell, I experienced a series of random events. Events like the dinner with famed CEO Jack Welch that almost wasn't, a realization of the severe nature of my son's illness, and working side-by-side with superstar Usher to help at-risk youth in the inner-city of Atlanta. Like I said, ultra-random.

How and when John entered my life is a study in manifestation all by itself. His presence and our partnership created a greater power than either of us possessed alone. John was a stabilizing force. He gave much-needed advice on dealing with Christopher, he financed much-needed medical procedures. He was patient. He helped Christopher enter recovery programs after a relapse. John was always there, except for one night in Roswell.

So we were in this large, beautiful home in a gated community with only four neighbors. While I struggled as a single mother early in life, in the years leading up to our marriage, I had established a successful corporate career, was making great money, and lived a pretty good life for a girl from Bloomington. When I was single, I lived alone. I traveled a lot for work, came and went at all hours of the night. I was a young female in a house with no obvious male companion for protection. I probably was an easy target, but when I was single, I was never threatened, never robbed, no problems. Fast forward a few years, John and I were in Roswell getting ready for a business dinner, and not just any business dinner. We were dining with Jack and Suzy Welch. It was May 4, 2009.

Our reservation was at the Intercontinental Hotel restaurant in Buckhead. I was sitting at my dining room table, gathering a few things together and speaking with Christopher before heading out, and out of nowhere — Boom!

Christopher's head slammed into the table. He was in mid-sentence, aware and awake with the side of his face resting in the palm of his hand. The very next second . . . he was out. Eyes glossed over with a faraway, almost dreamy look. I screamed and jumped out of my chair, shaking Christopher in the process.

"Christopher! Christopher?!"

I embraced him, kissing his forehead and yelling for John at the same time. Then out of nowhere, his eyes opened.

Christopher woke up as if nothing happened. The scared look in my eyes told him something happened. He looked embarrassed. Christopher hugged me and instinctively said everything would be okay. It was the strangest thing ever. We are about to leave for this dinner, and my son just passed out cold. Something wasn't right.

Now you have to understand when this took place. Christopher had recently graduated from college and was an intern with the Atlanta Chamber of Commerce, a nice job where he was making lots of contacts. Things seemed to be looking up for him. He was still quiet and reserved, reclusive almost, but nothing seemed terribly out of the ordinary. That is, until this fainting spell. Yes, he complained occasionally of physical pain — usually about his stomach, but that had been around since his early teenage years.

"Are you sure you're okay?" I asked. "What's the matter, baby? You passed out."

He assured me again he was fine, that he'd simply drifted off. He blamed fatigue and said he needed a nap. I stood there staring at him. I wanted to believe fatigue was to blame.

"Go to your dinner," Christopher said when he saw I was half ready. "It's important. Go ahead and go. I'll be fine," he insisted. My stepsons Tanner and Steve, and my son Chase were home, so I felt comfortable leaving. If they needed me, I was only a phone call away. If it hadn't been for Jack and Suzy Welch waiting for us at dinner, I would have canceled without hesitation. I didn't know how to feel, I just knew the night felt strange. It was the feeling you get when someone is there, but no one is in the room but you. The feeling that something has happened, but something else was *about* to happen. Cautiously, and prayerfully, John and I left for dinner.

* * *

Dinner was going well, but I kept looking at and listening for my phone. Suzy was delightful. We chatted and laughed. Drank a little wine. Talked a little shop. But I was uneasy. Something was off. Why did Christopher pass out like that at the table? I couldn't get the image of him collapsing into sudden unconsciousness out of my mind. I wanted to get back home.

* * *

A few hours later, we walked into the door, I immediately look for my son.

"How are you baby?" I asked, walking toward him fast with my arms outstretched.

"My stomach is still hurting, so I had to take some medicine," he said.

I thought I knew what that meant, and it probably wasn't good. He had been using again. That explained his passing out mid-sentence. It explained his appearance, and everything else. By admitting he'd taken some "medicine," I'd heard my son crying for help. At that moment, I knew it was time.

Atlanta is home to the Talbott Recovery Center. I made a few calls early the next day, and a representative said there was space available. Christopher could check in immediately.

"You know you can't do this on your own, Christopher," I said to him that morning. "You need help, and these people are the best. You're addicted to the medicine. You're addicted." We embraced. He didn't resist. He knew he needed full-time, round-the-clock help. It was time.

The next morning, John had to fly out on business, so my ex-husband David, who was in town, drove us downtown to the treatment center. I remember little of the ride, but I do recall the awful silence in the car. I sobbed, quietly to myself. *I was taking my baby to* rehab? The very thought killed me.

We stood at the door of Talbott. We hugged and cried. Said our goodbyes. It was horrible. Christopher would be entering a detox program, and unable to speak with anyone outside the facility for at least thirty days. He bravely accepted the protocol. I knew it wouldn't be easy. I turned, left the building and drove back to Roswell.

Back at the house, my son Chase started studying for finals with David tutoring him. As for me, I was exhausted. The fainting, the dinner, and now the treatment center were too much. I returned upstairs, climbed into bed and was asleep before I knew it. In the middle of the night, I suddenly woke up from a dead sleep.

My spirit led me to walk into John's closet and put on one of his long Indiana T-shirts. It was like wearing a dress to bed. My normal sleepwear was a short night gown that was somewhat revealing. This wardrobe decision will make sense in a moment.

I got back in bed and fell asleep. Out of nowhere, my bedroom doors flew open and a white laser light quickly scanned from one side of the room to the other. A man was standing in the doorway.

At first, I thought it was some kind of joke. My son Chase and brother, Roger, who was also in the house, were probably playing some kind of stupid game.

It was no joke.

The man rushed from the doorway, jumped onto my bed and peered down at me, resting the cold tip of a shotgun against my forehead. He had on a black-hooded sweatshirt with a ski mask. His legs straddled me. I was in shock. I didn't say a word. That's when another man entered the bedroom. He had a gun too.

My mind was racing. My unplugged cell phone was laying on the nightstand. I glanced toward it, which was the wrong thing to do.

"Get the fuck out of the bed!" the first man, the one in the hooded sweatshirt, screamed at me. I jumped to my feet, fully covered in John's T-shirt.

"If you say one word — *one fucking word* — we're gonna rape and kill you. Do you understand?!" I nodded that I understood.

"Get on your knees," one of the men said. My heart sank. *So, this is how I die*, I thought. Raped, robbed and murdered in my own home in my husband's shirt. I was terrified. I knelt down.

"Gimme your cell phone!" one of the men yelled. I pointed to the phone on the nightstand and one of the men grabbed it. The little light of my phone illuminated the room a bit more.

"Where's your purse?" the first man asked. I pointed to it, laying on a chair on the other side of the bedroom. He headed that way and opened it, rummaging through as he used my cell phone for light, pulling out my wallet and credit cards and whatever cash I was carrying at the time. He threw it to me on the floor.

"Give me *everything* out of it. *Now!*"

Without looking at either of them, I began handing them willy-nilly the contents of my purse — a checkbook, my day planner, a bill or two, a small bag of Kleenex, even loose change.

"Where's your safe?" asked the second man, interrupting my searching.

The question startled me. We didn't have a safe in the house. We'd never really considered buying one.

"*Where's your fucking safe?!*" the first man screamed at me. There was nothing left in my purse. It sat upside-down on the bedroom floor. I processed the question again, and as I did, I — mistakenly — glanced in the direction of the intruders. We made eye contact, and I remember thinking they would surely kill me now. That's what the criminals in the movies always did. When they know you can identify them, they kill you.

"We don't have a safe," I said meekly.

I felt the cold tip again. Only this time the long gun was pressed against my temple. And then one of the men began shoving me. He was irate, and it appeared I'd said something wrong.

His anger was growing by the millisecond, he repeated the same question.

"Where's the fucking safe?! *Where's the fucking safe?!* You've got a huge house — where's the *safe?!*"

I said it again, knowing I was putting myself in danger — but it was simply the truth.

"I promise you," I said to both of them, "there is no *safe*. We don't *have* a safe."

"She's lying," one of them said. I assured them I wasn't. The two began arguing with each other, one of them contending there was a safe and I was lying, as the other grew quiet and contemplative, seemingly more open to the possibility I was being truthful.

From behind, one of the men started pushing me again, this time much harder. I put my hands on the floor in front of me or else I would have fallen over. Unintentionally, I assumed an execution-style position. I stared at the tops of the shoes of one of the men. From behind, my face was being pushed harshly toward the hardwood floor.

"I swear to God, there is *no safe* in this house," I said. "We don't *own* one. But you can have *anything — anything you want,* just take it. Take my car. Take the TVs. Take whatever you want, please." I was begging for my life.

"Please don't kill me," I said softly, again and again, reaching for their humanity. "*Please* don't kill me."

There was a brief lull as if the two men were figuring out their next move on the fly. The first man, the one at whose feet I knelt at, spoke first.

"She says there's no safe, man," he said.

"Let's take her downstairs."

If it were possible, I felt even sicker when he said that. *Where* were they taking me? For *what* reason were they taking me downstairs? My mind raced with possibilities, none of them good.

"Get up on your feet then," the man behind me ordered.

I practically sprang from the floor. I felt another push behind me when on my feet, shoving me toward my bedroom door. The man behind me put the barrel to the back of my head, as if it to say "don't try anything funny." With the gun still pressed to me, I began to shuffle slowly out of the bedroom.

"Downstairs," the man behind me said.

Outside of the bedroom was a long staircase leading to a grandiose atrium of oak floors accented by a finely polished banister. They kept pushing. They were becoming more upset. I looked at the one that seemed to believe me and said again, "There is no safe in the house."

"Just walk," the man behind me said, and I did just that, quietly descending, one step at a time not knowing which would be my last.

* * *

At the bottom of the staircase, I was led to turn into the basement. When I did, I saw David on his knees on the floor in front of the sectional sofa. A handgun was pressed against the back of his head, too. We made eye contact but said nothing. I saw the terror in his eyes. He saw the terror in mine.

There was a movie playing in the background, Will Smith's western, *Wild Wild West*. The volume was blaring.

"Get on the floor," the man behind me said again.

"On your knees beside him." I took a position on my knees, on the floor next to David, when . . .

BAM! BAM!

Gunshots rang out. I covered my head, my face flat against the living room floor. I can remember thinking Chase was going to come downstairs in the morning and discover both his parents dead, murdered execution-style in his home. Then again . . .

BAM! BAM! BAM!

The gunfire was from the movie but the shots echoed in the

room as if it they were from those holding us hostage. Tears ran down my face. I was in greater fear than I ever knew possible. Then I heard Mom's voice, "Close your eyes, Cammie, surround yourself with white light."

I closed my eyes and a soft, yet protective, white light engulfed my very being. I felt God's presence protecting me. I felt an unusual calm. I was still scared, but I was at peace. I was bent over the seat of the couch with my hands against the back.

In moments like these, you think of everything and nothing at the same time.

Please, God, I begged, *Please save us,* I prayed.

"Where's the guy in the yellow shirt?" one of them yelled out. I knew instinctively he was talking about my brother, Roger, who was asleep on the third floor.

"And where's the kid?" the other man said — and I knew, *oh my God,* he was asking about Chase. From my place on the floor, I began to shake.

Not Chase. Not my baby. I would not lay there like petrified wood as these men sought after Chase. *They were not going to kill him, too.* I rose from my prostrate position on the floor and — with the end of a rifle barrel still pushed harshly against the back of my head — begged again, this time for my son's life.

"Listen, please — my son is going to panic," I said, trying to reason with them. "He's going to panic and things are going to escalate." By now I was looking directly at them, equally pleading and explaining.

"He's a teenager in high school. There's nothing of value in his bedroom, nothing at all," I said. "Please don't bother him or my brother. There's nothing of value in those rooms. Please. Please. Take whatever you want, but leave my son and brother alone."

One of the men was not swayed by my plea. He wanted

to go upstairs, remove Chase and Roger from their rooms, and then ransack the entire house. Somehow, though, a compromise seemed to be offered: they wouldn't bother Chase or Roger, but they were going to take whatever they wanted from my home. Both men ran upstairs, but before leaving, the hooded man offered a warning.

"Move and I'll kill you."

And with that, they disappeared. I could hear their clattering across the second floor above, turning over just about anything in their path, pocketing anything of worth.

Every few minutes, one of the men would return to glance at us, to make sure we were still cowering, then returned upstairs. They were obviously taking items from the house — and shuttling them to a car outside. Up and down, in and out — on it went. David and I laid there, helpless, praying to be spared, as the men made numerous trips throughout the house and outside to their waiting vehicle.

It was more than an hour into the ordeal when I realized it was over. Just as suddenly and as silently as the thieves appeared in my bedroom, they were gone. No announcement, certainly no farewell — just a sudden, eerie post-robbery silence.

David and I looked at each other, neither of us wanting to make noise or a wrong move.

"I don't hear anything," David whispered.

"Me either," I replied. We waited and waited. The men, it appeared, had not bothered Chase or Roger. They had taken whatever they could, and disappeared into the early Georgia morning. David and I collected ourselves. We sat up slowly, then stood, emerging from our execution positions.

"I think they're gone," I said. He agreed.

Softly — and with a great deal of caution — we walked

up to living room. There was nobody downstairs, we were fairly certain. As we entered the kitchen area, I could see the door wide open. I looked outside and my BMW was missing from the driveway.

After 15 minutes or so of walking through the first floor, David and I ventured upstairs, a truly terrifying prospect, not knowing what we might find awaiting us. We toured the second floor of the house too, slowly. It was apparent they'd taken what they'd wished from it and fled the premises.

That meant Chase and Roger were probably okay. I ran up the stairs to the third floor, where my son and brother were asleep — and as I got closer to Chase's room I started screaming his name.

"Chase!"

I ran into his room and embraced him. He had no idea what had just transpired below. I was crying and hysterical.

"Mom, what's wrong? *What's wrong?*" Chase said groggily. He'd slept through everything. I said nothing, holding him as tightly as I've ever held anyone, weeping from terror and relief.

"I love you," is all I could say back. "I love you, Chase."

* * *

Chase had no idea he'd slept through the home invasion. Roger didn't, either. As best I could, I began to describe to them what had just happened. At some point, I recall wondering why I'd remained so calm throughout the ordeal. I'm no badass, mind you. I freak out all the time over things like anyone else. But during the robbery — when I was at one point convinced of my inevitable demise — I never succumbed wholly to fear. By and large, I'd kept my cool. It might have been the only reason I'd survived the encounter.

In retrospect, though, I believe I was simply in shock. Nobody expects such a sudden, violent episode in her life, least of all me. Nothing in my life had prepared me for such a horrific ordeal. Yet the robbery happened — parts of it rapidly, and without comprehension, other parts in slow-motion.

"Don't rape me," I remember saying. I'd never uttered that sentence before. "Please don't kill me." Another first never said before. Throughout it all, though, I'd kept calm, like they teach third-graders to do during fire drills. I had spoken to the burglars in a monotone voice, one entirely devoid of emotion or inflection. No screaming or cursing. Almost businesslike, you might say. More like a zombie — a manifesting zombie.

But, in Chase's room after the robbery, I lost it. When I saw him sleeping safely in his bed, I fell apart, I wept uncontrollably in his arms. I felt like I'd broken into a thousand pieces.

"Call 911," I told Roger after collecting myself. He left the room and made the call. "Now call John," I implored him when he returned. I needed desperately to speak with my husband.

With John on the phone, I began explaining everything to him. He was in New York and was supposed to fly to London later that day. I could hear the concern in his voice. He said he was calling for a plane to get him home. I insisted he didn't do that. I was fine — shaken up, yes, but fine.

By the time my phone conversation with John ended, the police had arrived. The responding officers separated David and me, taking down our versions of the story. The perimeter of my beautiful home was secured with ugly yellow "Crime Scene — Do Not Cross" tape. Police detectives arrived with still more questions. What had been a terrible ordeal was now an intense one, as the cops scoured every room of my home for clues, fingerprints, or whatever might help them catch the two men.

A few minutes later, General Electric Security arrived and offered further assistance and ongoing protection. They took over from there. For the next month, I didn't leave home without an armed escort. I had no idea how this terrifying event was about to take another odd twist once they captured the burglars and we met, eye-to-eye, in court.

SCAN HERE FOR MORE

10

THE INVITE

After the police tape was rolled up and the Georgia investigators went home, I traveled to a place called We Care Spa, in California, to gather myself. At the spa, you don't eat, you just cleanse for, like, seven days. I was a wreck. If I thought I was going to die at the hands of those criminals, I was certain I would now die of starvation.

It was a beautiful facility, perfect for feasting on distractions — like steak and lobster — but instead, I was instructed to consume pressed juices. It was almost a waste of scenery. At least, that's what I thought at first.

The staff scheduled me to speak with an advisor. Her name was Renee. Renee was trained to address trauma. We sat down to talk and without spending any time on empty courtesies, she asked one simple question.

"What happened?"

I laid out the entire story, told her I was held at gunpoint and all the horrific details. I was just talking, and talking when she interrupted me and said, "Seems your husband does something really, really big, like on a global scale, right?"

I said, "Well, yeah."

Then she said, "I just want to let you know that what you're getting ready to do is going to far surpass anything your husband has done."

I laughed in her face. This was the first side-busting joke I had heard in a while. Maybe that's why I was there. I needed to laugh! It was all making sense. *She is obviously more than a counselor,* I thought. Renee was an amateur comedienne trying out old material on new patients.

"Let me help you out," I told her with a tinge of sympathy in my voice. "My husband is a well-respected leader," Then, I basically said she was full of the smelly stuff. After a few minutes, I softened my tone a bit because, after all, I'm sure she meant well.

"Love what you said, but not buying it," I told Renee.

"It's not for sale," she responded.

"Well, well," I thought to myself. These California folk are mighty free with their thoughts. In the south, we might just consider a statement like that rude, but I smiled and let it go. Probably because she did make me think, if only for a second.

Later that night, I lay in bed staring at the ceiling. It was silent, other than the sound of my stomach begging for food. That's when a single thought ran across my mind. What if the home invasion was an invitation? An invitation for me to dig deeper and live a more meaningful life.

Little did I know, I was about to join hands with, inspire and be inspired by those who held me at gunpoint. An event that nearly caused my death, was about to give me life.

This invitation was about to reach down inside of me and pull something up I did not know was there. I have always been a person who wanted to help others. I have always desired to be that listening ear for those who may not have one. But this event, this home invasion, would test my own personal resolve to be kind, to be loving, to be understanding. I was about to learn something about myself that I never knew. I kept thinking about what Renee said.

Maybe I did have something big ahead of me. My husband and I didn't compete, which is why we are perfect for each other. Once I stopped being defensive, I understood her words better. She was saying I am gifted to tackle something no one else has been able to tackle. That part resonated with me.

Marrying John exposed me to a different life. When we moved to Hong Kong, I somewhat recreated myself. I became more intentional. Before marriage, I was a successful single mom, working, and attending baseball games. I didn't have time to spend with charities or do much of anything else. All of a sudden, life changed. I started thinking, *Okay, I need to do something with the position I'm in.* Something based in purpose. I had more time and wanted to make a difference. I learned pretty quickly that I didn't need to be up-front. I had met corporate wives like that, and I wasn't one of them. I just wanted to do something meaningful, whether you knew my name or not didn't matter.

Even then, it was easy to doubt yourself. Did I have a voice? Who would even listen to me? I'm not Oprah, Dr. Phil or Joel Osteen. I am Cammie from Bloomington. However, I learned a valuable lesson. My voice is assigned to a certain frequency, just like a radio station. People who need you, can't hear anybody else *but* you. The radio of their heart is tuned to one station: yours.

I'm talking about the group on earth directly tied to the way you express an idea or the way you give advice. There is a group who understands that look in your eyes. They connect to the sound of your voice and the insecurity in your walk. Everyone has a tribe, and your tribe will die unless you allow your voice to give them life.

I learned that we are actually doing harm when we don't speak up and speak out. We are actually hurting people by being quiet. If you made it through all of your struggles, failures and difficulties in building a business or a family; if you survived all the gains and losses and even a home invasion, what do you think it was for? It is to inform the people behind you of the storm ahead so they will be more prepared than you were. I should stop being all philosophical, but the home invasion, as random and as terrifying as it was, had me looking at life a little differently than before. I needed to use my voice to inspire, and so do you.

I hope you never have a home invasion, but you will have an invasion of some kind. An invasion of your health, your career or your hopes. No one gets by without being disrupted in some way. Just know, your invasion will also be an *invitation* to live a more meaningful life. To be bolder about what is right, and to raise your voice louder so those who are looking for your station can finally hear your broadcast.

When I returned to Atlanta, my attorney said we had a court date. That's when I learned that the guys who broke into our home had done four additional home invasions in the area. In the last one, they stole the home owner's car. There was a police chase, and the SUV caught on fire. It was a disaster. Three of the men were caught. One wasn't. We started to realize our invasion was just random. This was what these young men did. We just happened to be home at the wrong time, if there is such a thing.

Right after the invasion, the detective thought one of Christopher's associates may have been involved. He took us all to Talbot to interview Christoper; what a thing to go through on your first day of treatment. He was mortified. Thank God neither he nor his friends were involved.

After that, everything happened so fast. I looked up and the young men who were responsible walked into court in yellow jumpsuits. I hadn't seen them since they were holding guns to my head. I was so naïve. I wasn't prepared at all for the emotions of this whole ordeal. The families were there: grandma, aunts, moms. I had to get up and testify. I looked at the boys. I looked right at them and said, "I do not hate you. I hate what you did to me, but I do not hate you. I'm going to pray for you." That's what I said to them. I told the whole story, the prosecutor asked me all these questions, what happened, when and how. It was a lot. The judge said "We're going to have a break." I got up and went to the bathroom.

When I came out of the stall, one of the boy's moms was standing there with his little sister. The little girl was crying, and the mom was just bawling. It was horrible. She grabbed me by the arm. "I'm so, so sorry. He's a good boy," she said. "He got with the wrong crowd. He was working down at a restaurant by the airport. He was doing good. I just need you to please forgive him. Please forgive him."

Then I started crying. Then I started bawling.

"I'm sorry," I told his mother. "I'm so sorry."

They hadn't announced a verdict or anything at this point, but she just wanted to apologize to me for what I went through. She thanked me for what I said in court, that I didn't hate her boy. Then, it was time to renter the courtroom.

The prosecutor started into the penalty phase. He said when the police searched the house, the boys had all of my stuff laid out on a bed. They had been bragging online about what they took from our home and the homes of others. The judge seemed frustrated. She asked one of the defendants a question,

"You did this to four houses?"

The boy just stared.

Another victim, whose house they robbed last, was also there in court. He was furious. The judge let him speak.

"I used to live in a house with a dirt floor. I work hard. You come in and you take what I spent my life working for? Burn in hell," the man said.

It was time for the verdict. The judge had the boys stand to their feet.

Twenty years in prison. No parole.

The mothers, grandmothers and aunts in the court let out gasping screams. I'll never forget the sound. Afterward, I sat in my car, crying uncontrollably. Seeing what happened to the families was nearly as bad as the home invasion itself. Their lives were over. Twenty years, no parole. They were 19 years old.

John was in DC, and entertainer Usher was there speaking in front of Congress about his nonprofit. They met briefly and following that meeting I was invited to attend Usher's charity event in Atlanta.

During the program, one student named "Dewey" gave a brief speech. As he spoke, he looked directly at me. He said, "I didn't know a way out, but now I am in Usher's New Look and am in college and no longer in a gang." The young man touched my heart. I knew I was in the right place. Fast forward, Dewey is like a son to me now. Ironically, I later found out that Usher and his mother, Ms. Jonnetta Patton, went into a juvenile courtroom years before and sat in the back, observing. That is when they decided to launch New Look, to provide a new look for youth.

From there, I joined the New Look board and was placed

in charge of its first major event. It was called the World Leadership Awards and included President Clinton and Justin Bieber. During the event, I had a chance to speak about the home invasion and how I got involved with New Look. There were easily — I don't know — maybe 1,000 people there. I think doing that really helped my mental state. I was working with the kids, explaining to them choices and how you can make one wrong choice and ruin your life. It still breaks my heart to know the boys who invaded our home were sentenced to 20 years.

SCAN HERE FOR MORE

Cammie &
Lil Bro Roger

Cammie growing up
in Indiana

Mama, Papa,
Cammie & Lil
Brother Roger

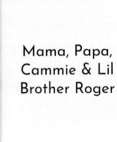

Five generations,
Lillian, Mary,
Charla, Cammie
& Christopher

Cammie loving
on her mother,
Charla

Cammie with her
parents, Charla
& Roger, and her
brother, Roger II

Chase, Christopher
& Pops

Christopher
& Emily

Cousins!

Critter!

Cammie at peace

Just Married!
Mr. & Mrs. Rice
est. 2007

Our four
Best Men

Aunt Cammie & Uncle John with their triplet godchildren, Hayden, Haylie & Harrison

Our Family. Tanner, Meghan, Lauren, Steve, John, Cammie, Tori, Bodhi & Chase

The Rice Side of the family!

Cammie's maternal side of the family!

The Wolf side of the family!

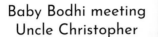

Cammie's gift
from God, Bodhi
Christopher

Cammie's son
Chase, Tori &
grandson Bodhi

Christopher & Chase's
Mama, Glenda

11

YOU'VE GOT A FRIEND

ddiction is a friendship. A person tied at the hip to alcohol, cocaine, opioids or any number of substances they have found to misuse, believes they have found a friend to cherish.

Words describing the toxic power of this *friendly* addiction can be found in candid discussions in rehab, in sober houses around the country and even tucked away in songs. But first, let me say this: opiates seem to have a different place among the hell of substance misuse. Of course, one cannot compare tragedies. One cannot compare what cocaine does to one family compared to what meth does to another. One mother's pain is every mother's pain. But I would dare say, if addiction was a chef, opiates would be its signature dish, served cold without care or concern for the lives it destroys. Now back to this "friendly" addiction.

There is a song, and a particular lyric that crystalizes how opiates can at first appear harmless. The song, "Fire and Rain," written and performed by James Taylor on his 1970 Warner Bros. album "Sweet Baby James," provides an insightful view into understanding opiates and its unusual power to make relationships with its victims. Opiates present themselves as a wonderful solution during your time of greatest need. In reality, it is the devil waiting to establish trust before thrusting a knife into your heart.

A young Taylor, who was fighting an opiate addiction, and grieving the suicide of a dear friend, wrote lyrics that used metaphors to express the pain, comfort and ultimate danger of becoming friends with opiates. Years later, he would recall his physician father giving him one last warning, calling opiates "kryptonite" that would eventually destroy him if not left alone.

Opioids as a "friend" is not a popular perspective. The medical and research community has done a great job informing us as to the chemical dependency involved with addiction. Words like dopamine and serotonin are nearly commonplace, but friendship? We don't often view the addict as being in a terrible friendship.

To that point, when I say the word *addict,* what image comes to mind? Who do you see? What do they look like? Are they educated, young, old, rich, poor, Black or white? Do you see a junkie on a street corner or a well-dressed professional in a corporate office? Do you see a rock singer or your local dentist? The reality is, addiction has no preference. *Addiction* is the purest example of diversity, equity and inclusion. No one is left behind. It only has one requirement, just be *human.* The drug will take care of the rest.

Calling this a *friendship* is in no way an attempt to soften the devastating blow to families who have lost loved ones, but if we are to reduce the spread of this epidemic — if we are to prevent another 100,000 people from dying due to substance misuse every year — we must process the problem differently. We must understand loneliness as a chemical all unto itself.

We must tweak our perspective such that we see drugs as more than a substance, but a person. What are the attributes of a great friend? A great friend is timely, they seem to show up just when we need them most. A great friend loves unconditionally. They understand us, reducing our anxiety by listening without judgment.

Addiction is a friendship. It's not the euphoria that gets you hooked, many opioid users say, it's the relief from everyday fear and anxiety, the soothing mellow sense that you're safe and nurtured and unconditionally loved. When you get that feeling — that artificial and fleeting, but nevertheless wonderful feeling — you don't want to live without it ever again.

Opioids mimic neurotransmitters in our brain, the same neurotransmitters that make social interaction natural, comforting and rewarding. Think about that. Opioids create the same feeling we get socially when a random interaction with another person is fluid and comfortable without effort. In other words, friendly. A person, who might otherwise be uncomfortable and shy around others, may, under the influence of heroin or opioids, feel familiar without any "social inhibitions." The most socially-awkward person can be the life of every party, as inhibitions and doubt disappear.

Opioids make you feel like you're loved. According to *Cigna,* three in five Americans (61%) classify themselves as lonely.[1] That's a *huge* number of susceptible lonely hearts across our society, so we shouldn't be surprised if many of these individuals act upon the human need to feel wanted, even if it comes in pill or liquid form. We know love is blind, and now we know love is addictive.

When patients leave hospitals after surgery, it's not

---

1 https://www.cigna.com/static/www-cigna-com/docs/about-us/newsroom/studies-and-reports/combatting-loneliness/cigna-2020-loneliness-report.pdf

uncommon to carry home a boat-load of opioid prescriptions. I saw this first hand with Christopher. Thankfully today, Narcan is sometimes given in addition to the opioids. Narcan is the true friend. It is an opioid antagonist used for emergency overdoses. It works by blocking body receptors to which opioids bind, helping to reverse symptoms of an overdose. Narcan reminds your lungs to breathe when they forget.

So if opioids represent a potentially deadly friend, how does one separate from its grip? That's the problem with addiction. No matter how hard some people try to get rid of their drug habit, the drug habit won't get rid of them. Imagine shaking hands with someone and then softening your grip because the handshake is over, but there is a problem. They won't let go. Sometimes we place the responsibility of letting go of drugs squarely on the person who is addicted, never realizing that the drug is also addicted to them. The drug has a chemical hand just like your physical hand, and just because you are finished, the drug may have a different idea. Letting go doesn't necessarily mean you have been let go of.

There's another side to the opioid problem. Many absolutely *hate* the way the drug makes them feel. Yes, that's right. For all the positive, "friendly" traits initially experienced, many people hate every second of it. They want to stop using because of the way it makes them feel, and this is where the chemical side of addiction digs its fingernails in even deeper.

Addiction is not only a back-stabbing friend, it is a disease, it is a personality trait. Studies indicate there are more people on earth prone to addiction than not. We are not only referring to loneliness. Many of us have a genetic trait making it easier to fall victim to substance misuse. This is interesting because we have no say in what our parents pass along to us. Have you ever seen a person avoid getting tall or avoid having green eyes? Of course not, because they have no say so in these physical traits. What if addiction was like height or eye color? What if our struggles with substance abuse go back to our birth, not our decisions as an adult?

I'm sure many of you are thinking, "Well, isn't that convenient?" and to be honest, I probably would have thought the same thing prior to going through my own personal hell with this disease. The reality is, substance misuse, especially opiates, identifies the tendency for addiction we may already have, and fills these gaps before we even know what is happening. We must expand our view of addiction if we are to ever have a chance at beating it. But wait, there's more.

Addiction not only seeks the lonely, not only attacks us through our genetic makeup, but it also attacks those who seem to have everything. Opioids seem to be more sociological in nature than drugs like cocaine, appealing to a certain demographic — a certain weakness, even a certain genetic makeup. You don't have be poor in order to become an opioid addict. You don't need to be unhappy, either. But there seems to be a social determinant at play that makes the drug more addictive to some than it does to others.

* * *

My own son's case proves an uncomfortable point, America's opioid epidemic was accelerated by doctors. Yes, started by doctors. In their defense, doctors were told opiates were not addictive. Many chose to believe it, some did not. Take a few hours and watch all episodes of *Dopesick*. It explains, better than anything I've seen, the entire prescription process. The drug use was fueled by doctors working with Big Pharma and trickled down to your corner drugstore pharmacist — everybody making a buck and looking the other way all along the way.

It is difficult to say this because we need doctors to help us solve the problem they helped to start. There are many wonderful physicians who have become an asset in helping the public understand the danger of opiates and how to avoid addiction. We are finally beginning to hold people accountable. The government is flagging doctors and shutting down pill mills everywhere. "Red flagging," they call it, when a doctor has prescribed an inordinate amount of opioids. Major courtroom battles are underway even as I write this, pointing fingers where they need to be pointed, finally. We are making improvements, slowly, but improvements nonetheless.

My son Christopher came out of surgery and walked home with enough OxyContin in his pocket to kill him several times over. I know a young mother who, as she was being discharged from a hospital after giving birth by C-section, was prescribed 60 OxyContin, despite not requesting a single pill. She protested and said she didn't need them — but was told by the attendants they were *required* to prescribe them for her. Why would OxyContin be required? Who required it?

Overprescribing is a big contributing factor to the opioid epidemic. This excess establishes dependency. Dependency creates destruction. That's what I saw happen with my own son. Because of his pain — physical, yes, and emotional — he developed a friendship with drugs. A friendship he so badly wanted to end.

His friendship with drugs took over, and elbowed everyone else out of his life. Christopher never had to worry about his next meal, paying the rent or if he could get new sneakers. He was not destitute. The world was his footstool. But once opioids gained a spot in his life, it held on for dear life.

He was the perfect candidate to become an opioid addict, but nobody told us. I'm sure, at first, my son loved how the drug changed his biochemistry, how it released that comforting dopamine feeling, a sense that everything was going to be okay. At first, it must have felt fantastic. Christopher was artificially happier, a lot less lonely and depressed, and for a while, he probably enjoyed getting to know his new friend in the smoky orange bottle.

The drug eased the pain and helped him forget. It lessened the stigma, real or perceived. The drug became his closest ally. It was always there for him, sitting right there quietly on his bathroom shelf, never talking, never judging, only ready to perform.

That day we dropped him off at Talbot, little did we know that every addict inside had their own personal friendships with addiction. It makes you wonder about the wisdom of rehab. Of course, many rehab programs are incredible, and Christopher's program would prove to be valuable to him, but the system of living all day with other addicts has much to be improved upon.

It's happening right now. Someone is being seduced by a substance as you read this. Someone is walking out of the pharmacy with the most powerfully-addictive chemical substance ever created. Or they're taking their first hit or snort. It's happening right now and the soon-to-be victims don't know that what they think will help them, has just made a down payment on their death — not to mention what it does to the family.

Addiction is a friendship. We would spend the next few years working, crying, begging and paying for this *friend* to leave our son alone. We were in for the fight of our lives.

SCAN HERE FOR MORE

12

STIGMA

This would not be a physical confrontation. Our family was about to fight an idea, an assumption, a stereotype. We were about to fight the invisible.

It started the day we checked Christopher into rehab. It was then I realized something: I didn't want anyone to know. I realized how powerful opinions were. Even the opinions of total strangers can influence you to do things you otherwise would never do. Opinions are dangerous because they make you hesitate when you should act. Opinions are deceiving because they are often not based on fact. You'll never see it written on an autopsy report, but opinions are often the cause of death.

It doesn't even make sense. If your child is sick, why would you care what a friend or family member thinks about it? Christopher is my son, and he needs help. End of story. That's all that matters right? Wrong. I took energy and brain power to create stories about where he was and what he was actually doing. I called his addiction everything but an addiction. I kept the truth a secret or at least massaged the truth so people never really got a sense that my son had a real problem. After

Christopher entered rehab, I vividly remember meeting with a girlfriend who had known me for over thirty years. Out of the blue, she asked me how Christopher was. I was at the crossroad of telling the truth or not. I had no reason to lie to her. And I sat there and told her that he was on a vacation with his girlfriend. I wasn't even willing to be honest with people who loved and cared for Christopher.

Maybe I was less than upfront with my friend because addiction can make you feel like you failed as a parent. If your child isn't doing well in school, hiring a tutor is socially acceptable. If they fail at a business venture, no one thinks the failure reflects on the parent, but addiction says something went wrong at home.

There has to be something you didn't do, quality time you didn't spend, advice you never gave. Maybe you were too lenient. Maybe you were too strict. None of this might be true, but it doesn't matter because opinions are still felt. You feel the judgment like carrying a tote bag full of bricks everywhere you go.

But wait, it gets worse. When enough individuals have the same opinion, it turns into something even nastier. Collective opinions transform into social stigmas. Talk about a mess.

Stigma communicates with you as clearly as if someone whispers their disappointment in your ear. It is as if the world knows you are free to be bullied. The stigma around addiction says, "Keep your mouth shut and deal with it in private." And that's how people die.

Stigma encourages those, who don't know anything about your situation, to assume they know everything about your situation. After all, isn't every addict the same? Every addict makes bad decisions, is irresponsible, steals from their family and lies about it, right? Nothing could be further from the truth. This became crystal clear when speaking to another friend about Christopher and his challenges right during the time he was admitted into rehab. My friend's uncle had also been an addict many years before. When she heard about Christopher's struggle, she immediately put my son in the category of her uncle.

I hated that.

She said her uncle was this and that — all terrible things, of course. I wanted to jump in and say, "But that's not Christopher, don't assume that just because the problem is the same, that the people who have this problem are the same. Good and honest people suffer from addiction just like good and honest people suffer from cancer," but something told me this would have been a waste of time and oxygen. My friend had made up in her mind that addicts were certain types of people who did certain types of things, and there was no arguing with her.

I had to accept the fact that people force your problem into their tiny box of misunderstanding. This stereotyping would be easier to take if it just affected me, but this is my son, and my momma bear claws are sharp and always ready. In order to keep the peace, I stopped talking about his problems to anyone outside of our family. But ultimately, this makes the situation worse. Silence places error on top of error. My son suffers, his loved ones suffer, his condition worsens and the silence grows. Stigma cuts in every direction. I enabled stigma too.

Christopher was never in any "legal" trouble. He never stole from me. Memories of that time keep me up at night. I have even had to address my feelings about rehab itself. At times, it seems rehab really helps, but it's also time to research new methods of treatment. One size does not fit all. What has become clear is that the power of words, the power of assumptions and the power of stigma applies to everyone, all the time. Even people in rehab.

While I fully understand the famous 12-step program used by Alcoholics Anonymous, while I understand why certain things are said, I would be less than honest if I didn't say I questioned some of the practices. Much like AA, those who enter drug rehab are taught to call themselves by their problem. I am aware of the sensitive nature of what I am about to say, but I'll say it anyway. How does it help to constantly call yourself by the problem you have? "Hi, my name is Christopher and I am an addict." I get it. Admission is the first step toward healing. What I don't understand is the teaching that a person struggling with a substance disease is supposed to call themselves by the name of that disease for the rest of their lives. Over a period of months in rehab, I watched the process destroy Christopher. The process designed to build his resistance to drugs began to erode his soul. Each time he stood up in meetings and said, "I'm an addict," It was the equivalent of saying, "Hi, I'm Christopher. I'm an asshole. I'm a dragon. I'm a shit. I'm a loser. I'm nothing. I'm nobody." His self-esteem plummeted to an all-time low.

What would be wrong with saying, "Hi, my name is Christopher and I am healed of my illness?" Think about that, "I am healed." Such powerful words of affirmation. Words that lean into the condition we desire for ourselves, not the condition we desire to get rid of. Words that manifest our future, not our past. We tell those who beat cancer to *say* they beat cancer or at least to say they are in remission. I'm a layperson, but it seems there are tweaks needed to the entire process and language behind rehab and recovery because, again, words have creative power and while we are reminding ourselves of the weaknesses we have, we are also giving fuel to that same weakness. Thankfully, the phrase, "I am in recovery" is also taught to many of those in rehab. I just believe we should do more to affirm where we want to go, not where we have been. The language and the vocabulary are so important. Such as "misuse" instead of "abuse" or opioid use disorder or substance misuse. This is to get away from "abuse." Seldom does anyone celebrate abuse. Let's use words we can use to affirm and encourage those suffering.

As you can tell, stigma, and finding ways around it, can take you down a rabbit hole. How crazy is it to try and describe the type of addict your son is? The type of addict? The very concept is insane. If a friend told you their son was diabetic, you would never ask, "Is he an honest diabetic?" They would think you had lost your mind, but again, substance misuse, ironically, suffers a unique kind of abuse all of its own.

What I mean by that is, the addict, their family and friends have to put up with assumptions, offensive conversations, name-calling and downright stupidity that no one else suffering from any other disease has to put up with. Thankfully, and here is the good news, this too can change with education and intentionally correcting errors when we hear them. Getting rid of stigma won't be easy, but maybe a good place to start is with this, "abusing drugs is what an addict does, but it is not who he is." Think about it.

If I'm gonna be real with myself, the change starts with me. I have to remove myself from under the weight of other people's opinions or society's opinions. I have to change the way I think before expecting others to do the same.

Stigma turns you against yourself. People who suffer from any number of autoimmune diseases know how this works all too well. Autoimmune diseases cause the body to fight against itself. The forces inside of us that were meant to protect us, instead work to kill us. Imagine that. How do you fight to protect you from yourself? How do you keep what is inside of you from attacking what is inside of you? And that accurately describes one of the most damning elements of stigma. What was once outside of you, in the form of toxic opinions of others, can eventually get inside of you, destroying you from within.

SCAN HERE FOR MORE

13

THE COPILOT

My anxiety reached Mt. Everest. Christopher needed help. My only prayer was that rehab wouldn't do more harm than good. I wouldn't say I was in a panic, well actually, yes I would. I'd heard horror stories about rehab, but I also knew of great successes. I was hoping Christopher would experience the latter. Stakes were high. His life and my sanity were both on the line.

You may enter treatment for one problem, but all your unresolved problems join you inside those four walls. And one of the unresolved problems that followed Christopher into treatment was abandonment. Abandonment by his birth father.

Almost as soon as the door to Talbot rehab center closed, I reached out to Ted. He needed to know Christopher was in treatment. The lack of effort on Ted's part to have a relationship with his son did major harm. Christopher needed to connect with Ted. Just as my birth father, Hawke, reached out to me. I know Christopher was hurt that Ted never reached out to him since he'd become an adult.

I tried to get them together. I did get them together. Once, they met in Florida fifteen years prior. I'll never forget it because Ted had a weird energy when he saw us. I just knew that when he saw Christopher in Tommy Hilfiger gear, maybe he didn't like that we had done okay without him. Even still, when Ted bought Christopher a pair of Oakley sunglasses, you would have thought he gave him a house. Christopher longed for his father so much that the simplest gift meant the world to him. Those sunglasses were like a pot of gold.

Over the years, when they tried to speak by phone a few times, each conversation was focused on Ted's other son, Christopher's half-brother. Christopher would always wonder out loud, "Why is he talking about his other son when he's on the phone with me?" And true to form, the day I called to tell Ted that our son had entered drug treatment, his immediate reply was, "I have so much going on right now. I really don't have the bandwidth." My heart sank. While I should not have expected anything different than what had been given over the years, somehow I still believed that, given the extreme situation, Ted would be different. He was not.

For Christopher, other unresolved problems came to light. During counseling sessions in rehab, it was revealed that he had been heavily bullied in middle school. All of those buried memories floated to the surface. I remember that time well. As a child, Christopher was a worrier. I never had to say anything to him about getting good grades when he was a young boy because he was naturally too hard on himself. He expected excellence. He was very book smart, but his health condition made him physically weak. His early childhood sickness was like a rip cord. Once pulled, it seemed to invite other problems into his life that otherwise would have never been invited.

At that point, Christopher had been in two treatment

facilities, but then had an ugly relapse. We were desperate and sent him to a rehab out west. Enter rehab number three.

They had a "no contact" protocol. When patients entered, they took their cellphones away. Patients weren't allowed to talk to their families for a while. Thirty days was usually the restricted time frame. To get around this, I wrote a letter, and a week later he wrote back. His letter was the saddest letter I had ever read. In it, he was trying to tell me the treatment center was not right. He was begging to get out. I didn't know how to exactly process what he was saying. Not as a mother, but as a mother with tough love. I went from crying uncontrollable tears, to holding back my instinct to get on a plane, ram through the front door of the treatment center and rescue Christopher. I needed to calm down. Maybe what he was experiencing was best for him in the long run. I needed advice.

It was Christmas, 2010. Christopher was still out west. As you can imagine, Christmas was miserable for me that year. Everybody was opening their gifts, and I just sat there thinking, *How's my son?* All those Christmas songs sounded sarcastic. All the lights, the gifts, the laughter, I wanted no part of it. "Jingle Jingle Bells, Jingle Bells" sounded like a chant from hell. I was regularly looking at my phone, checking the signal in case he called.

"Cammie, this gift is for you!" someone shouted from the tree.

My phone rang. It was Christopher. He was whispering, "Mom ... Mom, please listen. You gotta get me out of here."

Not long after this call, he wrote me a letter repeating his request for me to get him out of there. I took the letter to my spiritual guide. His name was Paul Gonyea. Paul was a retired Delta pilot, and a minister, the kind of man every family needs in their life. Balanced, compassionate and wise. He married me and

John. I asked him to coffee. The moment he saw me he could tell tears were hiding in my smile.

"What's wrong, Cammie?" he asked. The question was enough to buckle me in half. I was full that day. Full of whatever fills your heart when peace isn't there. I didn't know how to answer, and he knew me too well to beat around the bush, so I came straight out with it.

"I need to read a letter to you that Christopher wrote." He listened without interruption and then responded.

"Cammie, get him out of there. It's a cult. It's a cult."

I was like, "What?"

"No, seriously. Get him out," Paul said. I wasn't expecting that response, but with it, I moved forward. I got on the phone with the treatment center. The man on the other line was telling me to leave Christopher, and that he needed to stay put.

But in his letters, Christopher was saying things like, "It's abusive. They have us out in freezing weather." He said he could no longer take the conditions. "They aren't paying attention to my illness," he said.

I was torn. Wanting to act, having the confirmation from Paul that I should act, but still something in me wanted to know where we would go next. If he got out of treatment, how would he get help for his drug addiction?

I got him out immediately. The guilt I had was indescribable. I tell this story with a warning to do your due diligence when researching treatment centers. At the time, there wasn't a standard of care for rehabs. Do your homework.

This event started a cascade of events leading from Atlanta to Hong Kong and from Hong Kong to Cambodia. As I write this, I realize how blessed we were to have the resources for treatment. So many do not. This needs to change.

Yes, I should have acted sooner and I hate that I didn't. But there was still a problem. He was out, but his addiction to opioids wasn't out of him. He still needed help, so I began researching other treatment centers, again.

The next treatment center was called the Refuge in the middle of the state of Florida, near Ocala. The Refuge was very spiritual, had little cabins and beautiful waking pathways. He loved it. It was just the right setting, the right environment. We began to see progress. The Refuge was the best treatment center he went to. He was there for nearly a year in total. When he got out, he came to Hong Kong with me. I was so excited to finally take him to our school in Cambodia. He was better. We boarded the plane, I took my seat and prepared for a short nap. Pulling a small cover over my knees, I quickly dozed off. I wasn't asleep long when I was awakened by the flight attendant applying what I would describe as kind, but intentional pressure to my forearm.

* * *

"Ma'am, I need you to think!" The attendant declares loudly. "What is keeping us from landing?" Her eyes have a look not often seen in flight attendants trained to hide their emotions.

"What is unresolved?" At those words, I sit straight up. I am on a plane, but not the one I boarded with Christopher. The aisle is illuminated green. *This is that dream again.* The plane banks hard to the left. Glass and metal ring throughout the cabin. I can see the sky out the right window and also the ground out the left side of the plane. Passengers are holding onto armrests, others are gripping the seats in front of them. Everyone is scared. The intercom comes on, allowing us to hear sirens ringing in the cockpit.

What's that noise? I think.

The cockpit sounds like chaos. I hear a robotic, computerized male voice repeating a warning to the pilots.

"Pull up! Pull up!"

My God. What is happening? I haven't been in the dream for a while and somehow thought I would not have one again.

"Where is Christopher?!" I yell, still confused about seeing him only minutes earlier when we got on the plane. The pilot makes an announcement over the sirens now ringing throughout the speakers.

"Ladies and gentlemen, we are nearing the point of no return. All lights at each seat are green, all except 2-A. May God help us all as we are now headed toward the landing strip in Grudge."

At his words, pandemonium breaks out. Passengers who were encouraging me to remember before have turned angry. It is obvious we will all perish once we land in Grudge. I have never witnessed such fear. The screaming and the crying is unbearable, and it is all aimed at me. My light isn't on. I am beginning to pray.

"God, please help me. I do not know what I am forgetting. Please forgive every offense, every sin, every thought, every action I have ever done that was not in line with who you would have me to be. God, bring it to my memory . . ." *Bang!*

A loud noise, followed by screams, interrupts my prayer. A new siren I hadn't heard before starts to ring. It sounds more like an ambulance than something you would hear on a flight. The pilot comes back on the intercom.

"We . . . we lost an engine," he says.

Oxygen masks drop down from above us. The flight attendant holds onto my arm and my armrest as the plane banks. She struggles her way back to the front of the plane, breathing heavy. She straps into her seat, and with nerves in her voice, she begins instructing us on how to properly place the masks over our mouths.

"The captain has declared an emergency," she says. "Place the masks over your nose and mouth first before assisting any children. Oxygen is flowing even if the bag does not inflate." The plane is rocking back and forth, up and down. The pilots try to regain control, but we're in real trouble. I squeeze my eyes tight and, with my hands over my ears, I try to finish my prayer amid indescribable screams all around me.

"Lady, you have to remember or we're all gonna die!" a male voice yells from the rear.

"God, if you're there, please God, if you are there, help us. Bring to my memory what I cannot remember."

The cockpit door flies open and slams into the lavatory next to it. The sirens and computerized warning announcements that were muffled are now screaming with clarity throughout the entire cabin. The captain yells, "2-A! 2-A!" over his right shoulder as the copilot walks directly in my direction.

Only then do I realize I haven't heard the voice of the copilot the entire flight. Now, she is standing over me. A Black woman, regal in appearance, wearing a beautifully wrapped purple scarf. Her face is a mixture of sadness and beauty, as if she has been through hell and found a rose there. In the chaos, she kneels down next to me and speaks not to me, but *into* me.

"Cammie, my name is Ms. Tina. Listen to me, you hear?"

"Yes, ma'am," I say, crying and afraid.

"You must forgive for this plane to land in peace."

"But, ma'am, I have forgiven," I say while shaking uncontrollably. "I don't know what else to do. I've gone through each person I can think of. I prayed a prayer of forgiveness. No matter whose fault, no matter what the situation was, I have cleaned my heart."

"Have you?" Ms. Tina replies.

"I think I have."

Ms. Tina leans into my ear and whispers, "You have not forgiven everyone, precious. You have not forgiven yourself."

"Huh?" I don't know what to say. The thought never entered my mind. I am always looking out for others, giving mercy to others and providing grace even when it isn't warranted, but the one thing keeping me from true peace is forgiving myself.

"Do it now," Ms. Tina says.

I rear my head back toward heaven. "Cammie, you've done everything you can do to help Christopher. It is not my fault that he has suffered so much. I have given all I can give. I am free now to live without regret. I forgive me. I forgive myself."

The plane jerks forward as if we slammed on the brakes in the middle of the air. The entire plane gasps. *Bang!*

Another loud noise, similar to the first one, is heard through the entire cabin. All at once, as if all passengers see an angel, there is a sigh of relief.

Every passenger is pointing my way. The lady seated next to me taps my shoulder, signaling for me to look up. My green light is on. The pilot rings through the intercom system.

"Ladies and gentlemen, I cannot fully explain it, but our engine is working again. We are turning back to Peace. We have just gotten clearance." The entire place erupts in cheers and screams of a different kind. People are cheering louder than I can explain.

"Thank you! Thank you!" is being shouted from the rear. "You saved us!"

Ms. Tina rushes back into the cockpit.

"We are leveling off at 28,000 feet," the captain says. "We have enough fuel to get us to Peace. We should arrive in about 45 minutes." I wipe my face and drink the water in front of me. I am a total mess. The problem all the while was me. I need to give to myself the same grace I give to everyone else. Thirty minutes left before landing, I get up for the restroom. I turn the knob, but the door opens only slightly. I push and push, but something is blocking it.

SCAN HERE FOR MORE

14

THE PORTAL

When the prayers of family fill heaven's sky and the tears of a mother overflow into the lake of eternal grace that surrounds the mercy seat of God, a portal opens. This portal opens two days each year: the day a mother's child is born, and the day her child dies.

This is when God allows the deceased child to physically return to earth and ease the heart of their hurting mother, who has been living under the crushing weight of pain. This year, the portal opened for me.

Mom, this is Christopher.

Last night, as the clock approached midnight, February 25, 2022, I wept so deeply that my cries pierced through the sanctuary walls made of mountain diamonds. God, with an understanding touch, placed His arm around my shoulders, pulling me close. I cried louder, then louder. Angels and prophets of old began to gather. They wanted to see what caused the all-knowing to focus on me.

"Cry 'Christopher,'" God said.

Mom, He called my name.

"Do you want to go?" He asked.

For the past five years, I have avoided reentry. Instead, I have done what so many do here. We let our families feel our presence without physically appearing. I felt it would be too painful for both of us. We are so connected. We went through so much together. You and I were a team. Long before the family grew and my brother, Chase, came along, it was just you and me against the world.

You made sure I had what I needed, and I want to say thank you. Thank you for not giving up on me, thank you for not forgetting about me. Once opioids went from my body to my soul, it was nearly impossible to break free — but, even then, you never gave up. You never gave up on me. Death itself cannot break our bond. This year, I was moved to enter the portal. I was moved when I saw you decide to write this book.

The journey you are on, the airline metaphor to explain your pain, was not revealed to you by flesh and blood. God, who is rich in mercy, granted you this insight to heal bleeding souls. He uses creativity to shine a light of understanding into dark places, causing us to see our journey differently. You are showing the world that our days, our years, are not random. We are traveling a path designed for us long ago. Knowing who is in control gives us a greater ability to withstand whatever comes our way.

From the moment you started writing, I, along with a group of other children who died prematurely, have been watching. We read every draft and cheer for you from the balcony of heaven. From here, we can see all the lives that will be saved because of this work, but I want to tell you in greater detail how I came to interrupt your manuscript at this very moment. The portal closes in one hour, so I must be quick.

I may be upsetting the flow by doing this, but it's just that when I decided to visit, the first thing I told my angel was, "Take me to the book."

We entered through the tree you planted in my memory at the lake. I saw you printed out all the pages for review in your office. When you fell asleep, I sat there and flipped through each page. You may have noticed they were out of order from the way you left them. That was me. If the pages were wet, those were my tears.

In the notes, I saw there were several events you were intending to discuss before detailing the night I died. But first, let me thank you for discussing the physical challenges I had as a child. You were there each step of the way. Those years set the tone for my adult life. The ulcerative colitis, the botched surgeries, all the complications leading to them giving me excessive amounts of opioids for my pain, which opened the door to my addiction — they not only punctured my body, they punctured my mind; but again, that was a stop on my journey.

Thank you for standing up for me when the doctor came into my hospital room yelling, saying I needed to get out of bed, totally ignoring that my body was torn apart. I was bleeding; I could not hold my bowels; I was confused and scared. Thank you for grabbing his white coat and getting that doctor out of my face. You told the story well, but I know there is so much more you could say.

I saw in your notes, you have had so much loss: me, two years later your mom, and then the sudden death of your brother, Roger. When you started this book, he was alive; a few chapters in, he was dead. You were going to discuss more about our time in Cambodia. You love the place, and so do I. Mom, you are the happiest there. It is so amazing to see how extreme poverty is no match for the happiness of the Cambodian people. When we got there, it was, like, 150 degrees, and everyone was smiling! And we thought it was hot in Atlanta! You are at your best when you are giving to others. I can see why you say they make your heart sing. I know you want to talk more about that.

You wanted to write about how your guardian angels kept John from being home the night of the home invasion. I want to comment on that. Here in heaven, we see more than what you call "the future." We are able to see the different outcomes that would have happened if heaven had not intervened in your past. John was supposed to be killed during the home invasion, but God arranged for him not to be home. He has more work for John to do and assigned an extra team of angels for his protection. The security team from GE appeared, not just because they were called, but because everything on earth mirrors activity in heaven. The human team protecting you mirrored the team of angels protecting John. When the original scheme of the enemy does not work, they send sickness to the body as a backup to try to end the life they could not end. I know it was difficult to find out John had cancer seven months after my passing, but don't worry Mom; he is protected. Don't worry; he is protected, Mom.

You were going to write about that fateful day in Cambodia. How it started off so beautiful but ended with me on the bathroom floor blocking you from fully opening the door. I know you were going to write about meeting the Pope just ten months after I died. It felt like I was there when you met him, because I was. As you know, your grandson wasn't planned, but Bodhi Christopher being born six months after my transition is a gift to you from God. I'm honored he was given my name.

It's not an accident that on one wrist I was wearing the red Buddhist bracelet and on the other a Catholic saint bracelet Dr. Jenny placed on me, I'm still wearing them now. Remember the

Catholic and Buddhist prayer said over me? Each prayer represented my openness to receive God's voice from various religions, races and ethnicities.

I read your notes that you wanted to talk about the grannies of CCF who gave you the most precious, thoughtful and spiritual treatment after they heard what happened to me. Those women surrounded you, and, in a sucking-air motion, they inhaled the pain out of your heart, taking it into theirs. It was their way of saying, "You will not suffer alone." It was their way of saying they were going to help you carry the hurt inside of you by dividing it into several parts and passing it around.

You need to know that I watched the unbelievable sequence of events unfold as you and John tried to get my body home to Atlanta from Cambodia. And, finally, as I laid there in the belly of the plane for eighteen hours in that coffin, I watched you seated above with unending tears as you wondered whether I was cold down there. I was not, Mom. God wrapped me in His warm arms just as He does today. I know you could not grasp the idea of your firstborn being transported lifeless. It was beyond words, beyond understanding. It was other-worldly. It felt like fiction, which is why heaven inspired you to write this book from an out-of-body, other-worldly perspective. The more painful the experience, the more necessary it is for the story to create a new pathway of understanding — a new thinking approach that doesn't have the scar tissue of overused statements and meaningless cliches.

Mom, all of this was, and is, a part of your journey. It is a part of my journey. I would not have known any of this had I not had a chance to speak to God personally. I asked Him every question you can imagine. He answered them all. I am confident in one thing. He who has begun a good work in you will carry this work on to completion.

There is an entire division here devoted to you, the Christopher Wolf Crusade, and the efforts you are making to prevent mothers from losing children to the opioid epidemic. There are flight plans where mothers don't lose their children. God has given you this experience because you are now the reason their children won't be lost. I died so they may live. You live so they will not die.

Things that don't make sense on earth make all the sense in the world here in heaven. What I'm really trying to say, Mom, is, I am okay. I am okay with what happened. My biggest fear leaving you that night in Cambodia was wondering whether you were going to be all right. You need to know I had a choice, and I decided to leave.

God gave that choice to me. When a person is transitioning from life to eternal life, there is an opening — yes, a portal is the best way I can describe it. An angel meets you there with an outstretched hand. The angel seems to have on a robe, but it is actually her body. It is beautiful beyond words. Since God is the sun, everyone who spends time with Him glows. The feathers on this glowing angel are thick and soft, layered millions of times over. You cannot count them. When they flap up and down, there is a small but noticeable sound, think of the most peaceful stream mixed with the calming spirit of the ocean, then add to that the feeling of the sun coming through your window on a Sunday morning after a good night's rest. This is the soothing sound, the soothing feeling of heaven. You never get tired of hearing it. I call it "God's Radio."

When the angel saw me about to cross over, she asked me a question. "Are you ready?"

Seeing that I had never experienced anything like it before, I asked her a question of my own. "Will my mom be okay?"

"Not at first," the angel answered.

"What do you mean?"

"Cammie will fall into depression, disappointment and despair. She will nearly give up on life itself, but God will stand her upright when she can no longer stand."

This conversation with the angel took place while I was still on the bathroom floor. My eyes were closed to you, but open to me. I could see your face. I saw the look in your eyes, the profound devastation. They say hearing is the last thing to go, but, actually, it never goes. I heard every word you said. Most of all, I heard your silence. I am so sorry for hurting you. You are probably saying there is no reason for me to apologize, but still, I am sorry for dying. I am sorry for doing this to your life. I hate that you must live out your days thinking about me each morning you awake. Just know that each time you cry for me, I am here crying for you. We are connected even in our tears.

While heaven is perfect, it is odd how much you can miss the imperfect earth. Sometimes, I wake up with random memories, like making scrambled eggs with red peppers and sausage and then playing a couple of rounds of tennis with Alex. I know; random, right? I think of Chase and all he is doing. I opened a few doors for his acting career. Let's just say I put in a few good words with the big guy.

While opioids ravaged my body and mind, and while addiction got the best of me, the purpose of my life on earth could not be destroyed by that evil drug. In an odd way, opioids pushed me to my purpose. I would have never understood this when I was alive in physical form, but, once I got here, I was granted a different vision.

There is no imagination in heaven. There is no future, no premonition or intuition. None of that is needed here. All that is, all that was, and all that will be is seen in real-time. In heaven, there is no need for hope, ambition, or desire. All that is good is here now, every moment of every day. Time slows down when you don't anticipate it. Fear goes away when you know how things will turn out. What is left then is simplicity, happiness and contentment. We are free, each day, to watch over those we love who don't have access to this heavenly perspective.

The closest thing to heaven on earth is manifestation, and you have the gift, which is another reason you were picked for this difficult journey on Heavenly Airlines. In those early morning hours, my body died in hope, but my spirit awakened to all I had hoped for.

Your idea for a Life Care Specialist in every health care facility in the nation is the solution to what killed me. Neglect is the most dangerous drug of all. The Life Care Specialist provides attention and care. Thousands of patients' lives will be saved because someone will be by their side monitoring their pain and working hand-in-hand with their clinical team. But, for this to be successful, Mom, you must target the poor and rural counties of Georgia and across the country.

The opioid crisis started in rural parts of the U.S., and the solution will launch from the same place. Once the poor populations see the results of your program, the rest of the country will follow. Be prepared, because the growth will happen fast. I know this will work because, from my vantage point, it is already done.

Lastly, Mom, you would be shocked to see who is here.

People you thought would make it didn't, and people you thought would never be here are.

No one gets into heaven because they are perfect; they get in because God loves us perfectly. Even I — yes, even I — had some work to do once I got into heaven. When you were on the plane, trying to figure out what you had forgotten so everyone could land in peace, Grandma Tina led you to forgive yourself. What you didn't know is that your actions allowed me to do the same. After seeing what you did, I did something, too. I forgave Ted. Because of this, you now live in peace, and, finally, I rest in peace. Thank you, Mom. I must go now; the portal is closing soon. Roger and Grandma say they love you, and I love you, too. Today was a good day.

Love,
Christopher

SCAN HERE FOR MORE

15

WHAT HAPPENED

My dearest Christopher, I am so full right now. Grief can torture the soul, but, right when I was feeling overwhelmed, heaven provided just what I needed. I needed to hear your voice today. I really did. Thank you for loving me enough to come back, if only for an hour.

I read every word you wrote. I cried at each one. Since you've been gone, my days are filled with every emotion possible. Your death has changed my life, and I never thought I would say this but, given what is being done now in your name, you've changed my life for the better.

Learning what happened from your vantage point was so important. It gives me peace to know that you are resting in peace. It brings me joy to know that forgiving myself allowed you to forgive your biological father. The entire idea is almost too much for me to handle. Your letter provided a level of understanding that I had no idea was possible. You weren't forced to leave; you chose to leave. I needed to know that.

The night you died was entirely different for me than it was for you. From my perspective, there was confusion, horror and shock. And once we got you back to Atlanta, things got even worse.

So, when I arrived home, there was a message to call the local paper. As you can imagine, I had no desire to speak to anyone, but I wanted to see what this was about, so I responded. It was beyond interesting that people were attached to the fact you died in Cambodia. I sent an edited version of your passing to many people, and each time the element they latched onto was the fact that you died in Cambodia. It took me two years to be honest and open about the way you died.

But, in the time since your passing, I have learned to accept one thing: you are my son, and no one processes your death like me. For them, they hear the story and want to know the "juicy part." For a mother, there is no such thing.

"Christopher and I were in Cambodia to meet two Emory University physicians. We arrived the Monday before he died. Both of us traveled all the way from Hong Kong to get there. The reason for our visit was to partner with the Cambodian Children's Fund. For context, let me explain the broader connection. My husband, John, and I are supporters of the Emory Global Health Institute in Atlanta. Each year, Emory takes a few students from the law school, medical school, finance and business. They form a collaborative group of interdisciplinary specialists, and head out to a third world country to solve a critical health issue," I continued.

"The Cambodia Children's Fund is where we have the Rice Academy, where I've been on the board since 2012. When John and I lived in Hong Kong, I wanted to get involved in more philanthropic work. I wanted to do something that mattered for people who needed it the most. We traveled all over Asia and visited many orphanages, the Red Cross, and other charitable foundations, but, when I went to Cambodia, something was different. Cambodia was where I wanted to do my work. I felt it in my bones. But I never thought in a million years that it was where my son would make his transition.

"The Emory doctors were planning on analyzing the most severe community health concerns before having the students come over. I felt like we were missionaries, and I could not have been happier. The people there, the grannies, the children, the spirit and the smiles — I was home," I continued telling the story to the reporter.

"My niece, Bailey, was already in Cambodia working as an intern at the Rice Academy. On February 22, 2016. Christopher and I landed at the Phnom Penh International Airport, anticipating a meaningful stay.

"There's a famous bar at Raffles Hotel in Phnom Penh, the Elephant Bar. We checked in, and, so we wouldn't be late, I told Christopher to go down ahead of me to meet the doctors. When he arrived, he experienced a bit of shock. I remember it so well because later that night he explained what happened. Out of habit, Christopher had assumed when I told him to go meet the doctors, that he was going to meet two men. Instead, two women were at the table waiting on him. He was so embarrassed. They saw the surprise on his face, and he quickly tried to explain.

"'My mom did not raise me like this. I am so embarrassed!' he told the doctors. They were confused, not knowing what he was referring to. Christopher continued, 'My mom said we were going to meet Emory doctors, and, shame on me, I assumed you were gonna be men. Mom didn't raise me like that! To my surprise, here are two beautiful women sitting here waiting on us, and I'm so excited!' he said. The doctors began to blush."

Christopher, you were right. I didn't raise you like that! The doctors so loved your personality and having the honesty to say what you said.

I then explained to the local paper how I joined you guys in the restaurant, and how we talked about missions that could help the children of Cambodia.

"The next day, my son went to the famous Killing Fields," I said. "He put on headphones and heard all the horrible things that happened during the Khmer Rouge, and all the people who died. It was heart-wrenching, heavy stuff. When Thursday of that fateful week arrived, we were scheduled to meet with a senior government official. Christopher and Bailey took a few hours to relax and scheduled a massage. Before leaving, Christopher wrote me a note that I still have in my safe today. He left it on the nightstand. It reads,

"I went with Bailey. I'll be back soon. Love you."

The sequence of what really happened next, that I didn't share with the reporter, is critical. This is what I told the paper.

Christopher and Bailey go get a massage, but, instead of coming back to the hotel together afterward, Christopher left alone, telling Bailey he would see her later that evening. Now remember, this was the day we were supposed to go to a senior government official's house for dinner. Instead of going back to the hotel, Christopher went into the city and bought heroin. It was February 25.

In our research after his death, we learned he found a Wells Fargo ATM. It showed a withdrawal of $200. The next thing I knew, he wasn't feeling well and said he was going to skip the dinner that evening. I didn't know what was going on, but something was off. I had to run a few errands, but, while I was out, I also decided not to go to the dinner and canceled.

When I got back to the hotel, Christopher wouldn't answer the door. I couldn't find my key. So, I went back down to the front desk and got a new one. Upon entering the room, I walked into the bathroom. Vomit was everywhere. Christopher was sitting on the toilet. He was so sick. He was calling me, "Mom, Mom." He was sweating profusely. I was like, "Oh my God, what am I going to do?"

I remember turning the shower on. He was burning hot. Then, he was cold. I picked him up off the toilet and got him in the shower. I rinsed him off and called down to the front desk to have them clean his bed, which had everything imaginable on it. It was just awful. They changed his bed. I got him laid down, and stayed with him for a couple hours. I thought things were okay. All the while, Christopher was telling me it was food poisoning.

We found out later that, in Cambodia, the heroin is super strong. I had no idea. I don't believe he knew, either. Things were calm now. He was in bed resting, and I stepped out on the porch, speaking on the phone to one of the doctors who had traveled over to meet us. Every few seconds, I would peer through the window just to make sure he was okay.

"What do you think I should do?" I asked the doctor. "I don't have Gatorade. How am I going to get his enzymes built up? He's got food poisoning."

Christopher fell asleep and stayed asleep for several hours. But later that night, things took a turn.

He got up around 11 p.m. and told me he felt so much better. But, as it got closer to midnight, he was like, "Mom, I'm really dehydrated." He ordered some hot tea from downstairs. I was so tired from meetings all day and then taking care of him until midnight. He saw the fatigue on my face.

"Mom, you go ahead and go to bed."

When he said this, I was sitting on my bed next to the nightstand. Christopher walked toward me, leaned down, and placed his arms around my shoulders.

"Thank you for always taking care of me, I love you," he said.

Those are the last words I ever heard my son say. It was six the next morning, and I got up to go to the bathroom. I looked over, and his bed was perfect. The sheet I folded back was undisturbed. On the end of the bed, was the tray with the tea kettle. Nothing had been touched. I went to the bathroom door and knocked. Nothing. I came back and sat down on the bed.

"Christopher?" I called out carefully. I went back to the bathroom and peeked inside. That's when I opened the door a little wider and saw his foot. His head was on the baseboard next to the toilet. His body was keeping me from opening the door. I panicked and called the front desk to get the room number for Dr. Jenny.

"I need Dr. Jenny!" I screamed "My son! I need Dr. Jenny! What is her room number?"

They didn't understand English well, but they gave me her room number. I took off running. I'm was falling, running, and falling again. Once I got to her room, I realized she was actually right down the hallway from us. I started banging violently on her door.

Dr. Jenny opened the door like she had seen a ghost. I scared her half to death. "What's wrong?" she asked.

I grabbed her. "Christopher's out!" I said. "He's on the bathroom floor."

We ran down the hallway, into our room, and she saw him on the floor. She immediately put her hands on his inner thigh to feel his pulse. "Oh my God, oh my God, no, Christopher, no." She started giving him CPR. "Call the ambulance!" she said.

I ran down the hall screaming "Call the ambulance! Call the ambulance!"

Dr. Jenny did not stop CPR until the EMTs got there. It was nearly 40 minutes of non-stop compression. Her knees were black and blue, but she would not give up on Christopher. Once the EMTs got there, they would not let me back into the room. I didn't have a good feeling. Eventually, one of the EMTs came out.

"He's gone," he said.

Complete chaos broke out. Military people, the U.S. Embassy, the senior minister and his wife, Scott Neeson and Bailey — the room was packed. By the time they got there, Christopher was gone. I cannot describe the look on John's face when he learned our boy was gone.

A lot has happened since his death. In an unbelievable turn of events, I met the Pope, who blessed a rosary for me. One week later, something else odd took place. I flew to Sarasota to visit my mother. Because I met the Pope the previous Sunday, I wanted to go to a Catholic church. I had never been to a Catholic church in Sarasota in my life. The church was large, and several hundred people were there. They were having communion.

People came to the front row by row to take communion. I stood up, and out of the corner of my eye, there she was. "Dr. Jenny!" I yelled. She turned around, and we both ran to each other and started hugging and crying. Everyone around us started crying too. They didn't know what was going on, but they knew something special was happening.

We talked after church, as neither of us could believe that

the last time we saw each other was in Cambodia and then we ran into each other in Florida randomly. She told me her daughter was in a soccer tournament down there and that she had never been to a church in Sarasota, Florida, in her entire life either. It was just amazing. The woman who tried to save my son's life was now, in church, with me thousands of miles away.

"This is for you," I said, handing her the Saint Christopher blessed by the Pope.

"Oh my God!" She thanked me and said that out of all the deaths she had experienced in her medical career, Christopher's affected her like no other. She called her colleague in the aftermath asking if she missed anything medically that would have given him a better chance of living. She was assured there was not. Dr. Jenny and I are connected, soul to soul, forever.

That ended my interview with the newspaper. You can guess what I did and didn't share with the report. However, it was therapeutic for me. I smiled, I cried. Before saying goodbye to the reporter, I did provide two quotes from your funeral service, one from our pastor, Paul, and one from your brother, Chase. I love you, son. Please come back soon.

From our pastor:

Christopher was deeply interested in questions of faith. He was introduced to religion as a child, as so many of us were, but, when he went off to college, he began to explore. He began to actively search for answers. He studied Catholicism and Christianity and the traditional teachings so popular here in the south, but he didn't stop there. Throughout his life, short as it was, he read and he thought and he prayed in his own way, looking for a way to deal with the challenges in his life, especially his health. He had his personal struggles, as we all do, but he managed to grow through them. And, in the process, he expanded his spiritual beliefs to include other possibilities that worked for him in recent years. Because of Cammie's work with the Cambodian Children's Fund, he became interested in some of the eastern traditions, especially Buddhism. In the week before he passed, he and Cammie spent time visiting and chatting with the monks. The first thing he wanted to do when he got off the plane over there was to go to a temple. He began thinking about life and death in a deeper way. Christopher loved the idea that our time on Earth may not be the only life experience that we have. He thought it made perfect sense that life is a journey and, on that journey, we're going to meet people who love us and people who challenge us. But, most important of all, he embraced the idea that we are in this world to learn how to love ourselves and love other people. His religion, if you want to call it that, became love and compassion. He believed that was the message of all the great teachers, including Jesus. Love others as you do yourself. Give of yourself without thought of receiving. Unless you're like the little children, you will never see God. He believed all of this and more. The man who is going to speak next, Scott Neeson, showed up in Cammie's and Christopher's life at the perfect time in the perfect way, when they were healing from something. And, in the amazing work that he has done in Cambodia, he didn't know it at the time, but he provided a vehicle for Christopher to practice and expand his belief in the power of love. And it is truly fitting that Christopher's last days here on Earth were spent doing what he loved so much, sharing the very best of himself with other people.

From Chase:

So, this is by far the hardest thing, you know, our family has ever been through. And I want to thank all of you for loving and supporting Christopher, and my mom, in the interest of my family. Scott, Bailey, thank you guys so much for getting to her as fast as you could. And John got there as quick as he could. And thank you guys for getting my mom and my brother home safely. Thank you, Christopher Wolf, also known by his gamer buddies as Frost Ninja. He was the most unique person I've ever known — there's not a person on this entire planet I've ever met that reminded me of Christopher. He didn't feel like he had too many people he could relate to, but every single one of them is in this building right now. And I appreciate you guys. He loved all of you so much. So much. He had such a bright soul and the brightest smile. He's the type of guy that would hug every single person that he ever met, even if he's a complete stranger every time. He loved everyone and almost everything. He deserves to love himself as much as he loved us. He deserves to be as happy as he made each and every one of us, and now he has that. He never understood just how positive his impact was on people and how much love he truly spread. And now he can see it. I mean, Christopher, all these people, bro — look at all these people here. Christopher always wanted to be a healer, but he didn't know how he was going to be able to do it. Because of all of his traumatic experiences he had in the hospital, he couldn't even stand to be around it, but he wanted to so bad. It was his passion. And he was just trying to figure out and put the pieces together. And now his puzzle is complete. Now, he's a healer. His legacy is going to leave behind a health clinic in Cambodia,

Christopher's Hope, that will save countless lives for generations to come. Countless lives — and that's just the beginning. His death was a seed that was planted, from it will bloom so much life and positivity and love and family. That's all he ever wanted. Family was the most important thing to Christopher, unquestionably, and, Christopher, *you are the most important thing to us.*

SCAN HERE FOR MORE

16

GOOD GRIEF

I agree. There is nothing good about grief. Grief is a river, constantly flowing. Some days, a tsunami, others days a quiet stream. No one can predict how you will grieve. There is no pattern or system. A song, a smell, a color or even the cry of a child can send a grieving mother into uncontrollable tears. Grief is tailor-made to fit the depth of your love.

Christopher is special. I speak about my son in the present because while he is not physically here, he is still *here*. I feel his presence. I hear his voice. I'm still warmed by his personality. This is not spooky talk, this is love talk, and only a parent who has visited the dark cave of grief can understand what I mean. Only a parent forced to pick out a casket when you once picked out a crib. Only a parent who struggles to gather leftover pieces of a life ripped apart can understand. Our children never leave us — even when they are gone.

The effects of grief are unpredictable. One moment, you find yourself in a tiny corner crying all day. The next, you feel the courage to stand in front of a room full of people and give a speech.

This is because, grief wants you to know it is a lock, but it doesn't want you to know that it is also a key. The death of a child can eliminate the fear of dying. The fear of what others may think almost immediately vanishes when your child is gone. You begin walking around the earth like a wounded warrior, willing to take on any fight, win or lose. Grief is unpredictable.

Some parents sit at the funeral in shock, never shedding a tear, but then drop dead a week later from a broken heart. There is no plan. There is no normal.

After Christopher died, I remember cleaning out his closet, giving his belongings away to family and friends. Just thinking about it is making my hands shake. I remember driving to the bank to close his checking account, but I couldn't do it. The account is still open today. I can't close it.

If there is one thing that makes grief worse than it already is, it is people. People mean well but often say the wrong things, at the wrong time. For example, I heard things like, "God knows best," okay, well, yes. God does, but obviously, you don't say that to a grieving mother.

Some mornings I can walk by a framed photo of Christopher and smile. "Good morning my son," but later that same day I can walk by the same photo and break down. Unpredictable.

Grief is like a person, a person who hates to see you happy. If grief sees you having a good day, it will encourage you to stop by a grocery store on the way home only to hear a mother calling her son from across the aisles, "Christopher, Christopher! Where are you son? Mommy's over here!" Sending you running out of the store leaving the milk and eggs behind. Grief is always watching. Always daring you to smile.

People feel inadequate to comprehend what you are going through, because they are. It would be better if they were quiet and maybe squeezed your hand. So, then you find yourself defending yourself against foolish statements while managing your desire to faint each time you see an old friend who knew Christopher. It is a lot.

Add to this your own family. In my family, I'm the rock. My family expects me to be strong no matter what. But I'm also walking around, looking at my loved ones wondering who's next? I lost Christopher in 2016, my mother in 2018, and my younger brother in 2021. It's too much. You feel handcuffed. You embrace family and right in the middle of the embrace, you wonder, *will this be the last time I see you, too?*

Early on, I started to journal or post my thoughts on social media. Just looking for any kind of relief I could find. I wrote this message about grief.

* * *

AGAIN

You don't lose someone once; you lose them every time you open your eyes to a new dawn. You lose them again. As you awaken, so does your memory, so does the lightning bolt aimed at your heart, they're gone. Again.

You lose them over and over again, sometimes many times a day. Sometimes the loss, momentarily forgotten, creeps up and attacks from behind. Grief has muscles, full of strength to wrestle you to the ground once again.

There is no end to the loss, only beginnings. There is no number to the cost, only debt. You must learn to fight. You must learn to stay afloat when waves of grief threaten to push you deep. Be kind to those sailing this stormy sea, because one day you may sail the path now set for me.

* * *

I am a different person now. It's hard to explain. Christopher's death made me a better person, as strange as that is. Death makes you older and younger at the same time. You become bold and fearful. You gain a new clarity and a new confusion. It is as if the universe is playing a cruel game. A game you can never win. It seems all you need in life, is only delivered in death.

We've all heard the saying, a *part of you dies*. Well, it does, literally. It's the part that grew inside of you. The part you carried for nine months. It is a wonder that any mother can survive the death of a child. This is no exaggeration. It is a miracle. The pain is more intense than words can describe. It's like having a heart attack, a stroke, being tortured then run over by a Mack truck all before breakfast. If you are a person who doesn't believe in God, the fact that a mother doesn't die the moment she learns her child has died should convince you of a higher power. No one is strong enough alone to survive this.

God is the only way I made it on February 26, 2016, and God is the only way I continue to make it each and every day. One cliche is *not* true, time does not heal. Time is a prosthetic. When a person loses an arm, a prosthetic can serve to make them partially functional again. Prosthetics don't heal. A person may get by, but the natural arm, the God-given arm, is never coming back. Time teaches you how to operate at a loss, but your arm is never coming back.

That is the truth about grief. There is no way you can sugarcoat it. There is no nicer way to talk about the worst thing that can happen to a parent. No class, no group and no book are going to bring your precious child back into this world, but here is the irony, once you admit this, something happens. If there is anything that makes grief better, it is truth.

Saying truth, listening to truth and only spending time

with people who will tell you the truth can bring you to a place of peace. Truth also makes you realize something else: most people never hear it. If there is any, even a tiny silver lining in losing my Christopher, it is this: I see other people suffering and I give them notes for their journey. Like a tour guide in hell, I can show them where the ice water is. How to manage people and provide suggestions to protect their sanity. Before you can change the world, you have to lose yours.

Before you can touch the deepest parts of the human spirit, the deepest parts of yours must be torn in two. I wish this weren't the case, but it is. I wish I could help those who are hurting, and those who have suffered loss without having participated in the same fate, but I have learned this is impossible. Before you teach, you must first learn.

If you are reading this and tears are threatening to fall, let them fall. If you feel like giving up, give up — but only, for a moment. Step aside, stop being strong, allow yourself to bleed so you can fight another day. The sun sees everything, but it still shines. Go outside, stand under its rays. Soak in its energy. Smile and cry, cry then smile. Walk then run, run then walk. Give yourself permission to be quiet without caring what others may think. Let your body breathe at the pace it wants to. Then turn around and grab the hand of a grieving parent behind you. Pass along to them the small doses of joy you have found. Ask about their child, and watch the light reenter their eyes. Because if there is anything that can heal, it is the one thing grief can't steal: our memories.

SCAN HERE FOR MORE

17

A MISSING PEACE

I t was April of 2017. My son had passed. We were back in Atlanta from Hong Kong, and I was wondering how I might find some meaning in this tragedy. I replayed the last 20 years over, and over and over again. I thought about what I would have done differently. I thought about what might have helped me be a better mother, caregiver and protector of Christopher. I thought about what I know now, and what I didn't know then.

I needed more information when Christopher was hospitalized, not just about the drugs he had been prescribed and the danger they presented, but also about the importance of treating his anxiety and overall trauma related to his surgeries. Since then, I've learned that about 10 million people in the U.S. misuse prescription opioids annually, and about one-half of these people also suffer from a co-occurring disorder (i.e., anxiety, depression, post-traumatic stress disorder). Of those suffering from both substance misuse and a co-occurring disorder, 2.5 million have received no treatment at all, and only 6% (!) received treatment for both conditions. I'm not a doctor, but it seems to me that attempting to address substance misuse without recognizing and treating accompanying co-morbidities is a "prescription" for failure.

Prescription opioids are an important weapon in the medical arsenal for treating chronic pain and facilitating rapid recovery from surgery and other traumatic injuries. But prescription opioids can also lead to bigger problems, as 80% of all individuals who have used heroin reported first misusing prescription opioids. In 2001, The Joint Commission, a steward of quality and safety in health care settings, introduced pain management standards, which helped establish pain as the "fifth vital sign." Then it was off to the races, with the medical community and their patients focused on a pill and a quick fix to eliminate pain. Effectively, pain "management" had become pain "elimination," with minimal regard for the downstream impact from regular or prolonged use of opiates, even when the risk of addiction was more fully understood.

Treatment in recovery for people suffering from substance misuse disorders can be effective, but it doesn't always work, as was the case with Christopher. It is usually programmed around a 30-day cycle because that is how long insurance coverage (for the 20% that have it) lasts. Many experts feel that at least 90 days of treatment is required to establish a real path for recovery. Regardless, the point is this: once you have an opiate-related substance use disorder, recovery becomes a challenge that lasts a lifetime, or when unsuccessful, takes a life. That is why John and I decided to form CWC Alliance (aka Christopher Wolf Crusade) in 2018 to focus on education and prevention. At that point, I needed something, anything, to find some meaning in Christopher's death.

Setting up our own nonprofit was an interesting process.

I made John the chief financial officer, with a job description that restricted his use of the word "no." From the beginning, our focus was to establish a position for adults in hospital situations that would provide opiate education and alternative pain management strategies for patients and their caregivers. In pediatric hospitals, the analogous role is "Child Life Specialist," and today there are approximately 6,000 of these positions in children's hospitals throughout the U.S. I was first introduced to this concept by Jane Miller, CEO of Alliance for Kids. I then learned from Donna Hyland, CEO of Children's Hospital of Atlanta (CHOA), about how effective the role was at CHOA, and also about how there was nothing in place to provide similar assistance to patients who were admitted into general or adult hospitals. This was the same situation Christopher and I faced 25 years ago. Too many questions, and no one with enough time, or knowledge, to answer them.

So, CWC was off and running, but we started sprinting after I met Dr. Mara Schenker when she spoke at a conference I attended in 2019. Actually, I stalked her after the conference ended, and told her briefly about what CWC was doing. Mara is the chief of orthopedics at Grady Hospital in Atlanta, one of the busiest level one trauma hospitals in the country. She also heads the trauma division for Emory University School of Medicine. Mara spoke about the opiate epidemic and there was something about what she said, and how she said it, that made me want to get to know her better.

Mara and I had lunch a few weeks later, and things really started to click. She was very enthusiastic about the Life Care Specialist (LCS) concept, and we both thought it made sense to start in an orthopedic trauma unit — which is where many patients receive opiate prescriptions for pain. In many cases, a "first exposure" to prescription opiates follows an athletic injury, car accident, etc. without any conversation about the dangers that come with the prescription. In fact, Mara later told me that she was surprised to learn that her unit had among the highest opiate prescribing rates at the hospital and that patients often treated prescription opioids like a negotiation. As she put it, "We don't let them negotiate dosage amounts for other medications like antibiotics, so why do we do it with opiate pain medication?"

Our first LCSs started at Grady in the orthopedic trauma unit in 2020, working with patients who were in severe pain, in coordination with their doctors, nurses, and other members of the healthcare team. They introduced patients to alternative pain-management strategies, educated them (and their caregivers) regarding opiate use and the risk of addiction, and evaluated patients for other factors which could suggest an increased risk for subsequent substance misuse.

With Mara and a great team of researchers and LCSs, the position became effectively a hybrid between a behavior-based pain coach and substance use disorder counselor. LCSs provide evidence-based pain management education, perform opioid risk assessments, and coordinate care management. This includes harm-reduction strategies and follow-up after discharge at the two-, six- and twelve-week intervals. There is a particular focus on mental wellness using models that were developed by the Trauma Resource Institute, teaching techniques to deal with anxiety, stress, depression and PTSD. CWC continues to research new and innovative ways to cope with pain.

Creating a new position in healthcare required data, so we launched a two-year clinical trial, which has just been completed. Early results are promising, with a 25% reduction in opiate utilization among the patients being seen by an LCS, and a 30%

referral rate for other issues including food and housing insecurity, domestic violence, etc.

At the beginning of this journey, we had no idea how many additional problems we would uncover, but spending time with patients allowed us to build trust and discover these other potential problems that might have been overlooked. We are committed to keeping the role sustainable, scalable and affordable. Providing scientific data is important but now it is time to focus on the human side, and save lives.

SCAN HERE FOR MORE

18

FLIGHT 918

It's 6 a.m. I've been up since four. Something's in the air. Not because it's quiet. It's aways quiet this time of morning. But because it's thick. The air is thick. The ninth month is always full. Full of memories mixed with smiles, and smiles that turn to tears. Still, something feels different. It is September 18th, Christopher's heavenly birthday.

The book you are reading is being launched this evening on the campus of Emory University. I poured blood, sweat and tears onto these pages for the last 18 months. All 18 chapters were completed on the June 18. The timing of this project was controlled by something much bigger than me. The results of this work will be far greater than anything I could have planned. I am a participant and an observer. You are a reader and a solution. We are on this journey, together.

This process taught me how difficult it is to talk about the hell you've been through, and I mean to really talk about it, not the sanitized version that places you in the best light. There is a tendency to sugarcoat sour things so our pride can keep standing tall. I learned early on, not to do that. I learned if I was having an emotional breakdown, to call it just that. To say things as they are, not as I wished they were. Drug abuse, drug misuse, addiction and overdose is bitter. Fentanyl deaths are not overdoses, it is poison in a pill. It is murder. So, if you're going to talk about it, say it all or say nothing at all.

When you commit to being honest, you find the power to do what has never been done. Tonight, I will do what I've never done when we gather on the campus of Emory University. By "we" I mean family, friends, business associates, and medical professionals. We will laugh. We will cry. We will strategize on how to get the word out about the Life Care Specialist, and at the same time, renew our vow to put a stop to this opioid epidemic. But I must say, my emotions are all over the place.

It just so happens to be the perfect day for that. The sky is overcast. There is a slight mist of ran, but the sun is peaking through the clouds. It all makes sense. Sometimes, everything happens at once. Sometimes the sun and the rain occupy the same space. While I'm excited, I just hope I can make it through the night. Whenever I see Christopher's picture on a large screen, it does something to me. On the inside, I am filled with joy, but also sadness and grief, in other words, the sun and the rain occupy the same sky.

The planning and resources required to organize tonight's book launch is all because of a tragedy. While I would like to position things differently in my mind, the fact still remains. We are here, we are doing what we are doing, and I have written what I wrote because Christopher is gone.

So even though millions will be positively affected because of the loss my family has endured, in the end, we would much rather just have him back. We would rather not look at an empty seat at our dinner table or be tearfully reminded of his beautiful optimism while flipping through his childhood drawings.

Cammie, accept what you cannot change, focus on what you can. That's what I tell myself. With every creative bone in my body, I have to do all I can to stop the havoc caused by opioids. Christopher deserves nothing less. Honoring his memory means keeping people alive.

Tonight's program will be a combination of research and testimonies on the dangers of opioid misuse. We will read chapter one of this book, along with enjoying great music and gifts for all in attendance. I will be interviewed and asked the reasons why this project is so important to me. My heart is heavy, but I don't want tonight to be a sad occasion. I want everyone to leave optimistic about the power we all have to change the world. I've invited a few hundred people, and I am hopeful all the RSVPs will show up. I have a good feeling they will.

It is 2 p.m. There are a few details yet to be completed. No matter how honorable the program, certain basic tasks must be done. I had to make sure the food, the lighting and the aesthetic fits the program just right. We considered having alcohol served, but decided against it. Somehow, speaking about the danger of drug misuse didn't seem in harmony with passing out dirty martinis. Each attendee will receive a tote bag with one book, along with other various mementos of tonight's event. Dr. Mara will be speaking. She will detail the success of our clinical trials. We are in talks with several hospitals who are interested in welcoming the Life Care Specialist into their ranks of care. We need every heart, and every hand from every walk of life.

It is 4:30. The launch is less than three hours away, and I'm considering what to wear. Yes, of course, I had an entire outfit already planned, but I've changed my mind. I want to be a bit less stuffy. My closet looks like midnight because everything is black, but I think I'm going to wear purple. I am very much aware that, at any moment tonight, I could burst into tears. A smell, a color, the sound of a laugh or even seeing that look in the eyes of family friends who know what I'm feeling can send me off the rails. It doesn't take much, so I want to feel comfortable crying, if that makes any sense.

The things you have to think about when the unthinkable happens. You have to wear crying clothes. Thankfully, John will be with me every step of the way. We will drive separately as I need him to pick up everything I forgot to pick up and deliver to the venue. He is my rock, and tonight I'm gonna need the stability. One second, my phone is ringing. I don't recognize this number.

"Hello?"

"Ms. Cammie?"

"Yes?"

"We have a problem."

"Who is this?

"This is James. I am the facility coordinator at Emory in charge of your event tonight."

"Hi, James, what's the problem?"

"We have no power."

"Excuse me?"

"The auditorium has no power. The transformer blew a few minutes ago. We contacted Georgia Power. They assured us it'll be fixed today, but cannot guarantee what time."

"Well, that's not good."

"I know, Ms. Cammie. Just wanted you to know what's going on because it is already a quarter to five."

"What are the options to get everything back on just in case the power company is running late?"

"We have a generator that can give basic power to the

building. We can also use the recessed lighting and the emergency flood lights in the building, if necessary. All the entry doors need power to open so there's that."

"This can't be happening."

"I know, Ms. Cammie. But, let me run and get back on the phone with Georgia Power to make sure they are on top of this with all deliberate speed. I'll keep you updated."

"Thank you, James. If you can't reach me, call my assistant, Anna, and she'll get me the message. I just texted you her number."

"Okay, talk later."

"Bye."

I need to call John.

"Hey, honey."

"John, you won't believe what happened. The auditorium at Emory has no power."

"How is that possible? What are you talking about? We were just there this morning."

"Some transformer blew. The facility guy called. They're working on it, but Georgia Power doesn't know if it'll be fixed in time for tonight."

"Well, Cammie. It has to be fixed by tonight. There is no other option."

"I know."

"Give me the guy's number who called you. Let me speak to him. Everything will be fine. I'll make sure of it."

"Thank you, dear. Thank you so much. I am so stressed right now. I'll text his number. Love you."

"Love you, too. Bye."

It is 5:15. My doorbell rings. It's my hairdresser. I've already gotten my hair done but she's just handling some last minute touches. We take a seat in front of my vanity mirror. I'm frantically on the phone for the next thirty minutes calling my assistant and everyone else. We don't need any other issues. The power is enough.

Everything else seems to be moving smoothly. We have people flying in from all over the country. Many of the Emory board members will be attending, along with CWC donors, local political and business leaders. We need power. We have to have power. What are the chances of this happening today? Out of 365 days, the transformer blows today?

I sat in front of the vanity covering myself in white light. I did what I've done since childhood. I need more than electrical power, I need power from a higher source.

It is 5:45. Anna, and I are driving to the venue only twenty minutes away. My phone rings. I put the call on Bluetooth.

"Hello?"

"Ms. Cammie, James here. The power isn't back on yet so the maintenance crew hooked up two generators to the building. We have partial power, but not all power."

"What will we be missing, James?"

"We won't have house lights, but we'll have the recessed lighting I was telling you about earlier, and also the emergency floodlights."

Anna looks over at me with absolute fright. She alone, with a team of about ten volunteers, have been diligently working on every detail for tonight's launch. Because of the theme of this book, the greeters at the door will be dressed in airline flight attendant uniforms. Think Delta. Everything, down to their shoes and the buttons on their collars will make you think you are entering an aircraft. Not having lights will certainly destroy all we have worked on. The look on her face said all of that.

"Ms. Cammie? Ms. Cammie? Are you there?

I had gone off into a daze, still trying to understand how this problem could actually be happening.

"Yes, James, I'm here."

"Your husband is talking to the crew now and trying to figure out a better solution."

"Okay, are people showing up?"

"A few cars, yes."

"Is there air conditioning?

"Yes, ma'am. We have one generator dedicated to the air so the auditorium is cool."

"Okay, okay. We will see you in a few minutes."

Frantically, Anna and I play around the edges of the speed limit to get to the Emory campus. Other team members are there waiting. Volunteers are in place, the musicians, the children in CWC shirts are lined up outside, and the professional narrator who is reading chapter one just sent me a text saying, "I'm here."

It is 6:15. We pull up to the auditorium parking lot to find a Georgia Power truck out front. Crews are climbing the pole. The show must go on. When I step out of my car, I'm greeted with smiles and hugs from my staff. From a distance, a man approaches in a khaki jumpsuit. This must be James.

"Ms. Cammie, you'll be able to start and we'll keep working on it. As soon as everything is back up we'll just hit the switch."

I took a step back and looked around. Aside from the large white truck outside, no one should know anything is out of place. Then, I walked into the auditorium. I couldn't believe my eyes. With the main lights off, and just the recessed lighting showing there was a certain calm like when you board an evening flight.

You couldn't have planned it but, the way the flood lights hit the interior decoration, the purple and the white accents created what I can only describe as perfection by mistake.

Because the sun had not set, we were getting natural golden hour light through the windows. The auditorium looked incredible. I could not believe my eyes.

It is 6:45. The small cello quartet begins to play. Guests are filling the aisles. There is a feeling I can only describe as a symphony hall energy right before the conductor taps her wand snapping the musicians to attention. One would think, the low lighting was a part of the plan, and now I'm starting to think it was. The generators are far enough in the back where you can't hear them running. The audio system is working. Everyone who is on program is lined up in the back ready to go. I have no idea when the full power will be on, but it's show time.

It is 7 o'clock. The narrator steps to the microphone, and with a weathered, authoritative voice announces, "Welcome Onboard. Welcome to The Flight."

The audience erupts into applause. He provides a moment, then quiets their sizzle with the book's opening.

* * *

One day God decided to launch an airline. Every city will be serviced, every airport is convenient. You can fly anywhere your heart desires, and while you may not arrive on schedule, you will always arrive on time. There's one thing that separates God's airline from its commercial competitors. Every ticket is free, but it will cost you everything.

* * *

You could hear an ant wearing slippers crawling on velvet. It was more than quiet. It was still. Perfectly still. By the time the first chapter was completed, the table was set. The program moved in such a fluid manner, I nearly forgot we had no power — because we did. Everyone felt it. The power was in the words, in the conversation, in our shared experiences, and in our shared commitment to end this epidemic.

An hour and a half later, the program concluded with the passing out of the book. Attendees were holding onto it like a piece of gold, promising to share it with everyone they knew. Oh, and yes, halfway through the program, the full electrical power was restored. No one knew it was ever gone. Behind the scenes, Georgia Power saved the night.

After greeting everyone who attended, we began to file out of the auditorium feeling like we had just taken a trip, because we had. John and I could not have been prouder. We kissed and promised to meet back at the house for a debriefing of the night. As I'm walking to my car, James catches up to me.

"I didn't hear it all, but I heard some of the program. May I have a book?"

"Of course you can," I answered.

Placing my bag on the ground, I reached to the bottom for an extra book. When I looked up to hand the book to James, he had tears in his eyes.

"Thank you," he said.

"No, thank you, James."

He tucked the book under his arm and quickly walked away. *That's interesting,* I thought to myself. I approached my car thinking about the night, thinking about what was next, thinking about James. It is 9:07.

For some reason, a parked car is peaceful. I sat in mine for a few minutes. Today has been a whirlwind. Time to go home. All I can think about now is crawling into my bed and going over the program with John. I push the start button, but nothing happens.

"Mmmm." I press the button again. The internal lights come on, but the engine doesn't turn over. I tried again, and again. Nothing. My car won't start. I looked around to see a few security guards. I parked in a secured lot when the Georgia Power truck took over space in front of the auditorium. John will be home in a few minutes. If I call, he'll turn around immediately and come get me, but since the car is secure and whatever is wrong won't be fixed tonight, I decided to Uber.

I open the app and request a vehicle. It is 9:14. Four minutes later, my car arrived. The driver's name was Destiny. A beautiful young woman probably in her early thirties with a bit of a bohemian vibe.

"Are you Cammie Wolf Rice?" she asked when I opened the back door.

"I am." This was the first time a driver has called my full name, but maybe it's an update to the app.

"Okay, let's go," Destiny said. "Been driving since four this morning. This is my last trip."

We took off and headed toward Highway 85. For the first five minutes we chatted a bit, but her comfortable seats, the spa-like music she was playing and the soft gardenia fragrance in the car, had me dozing off.

I was awaken by what seemed to be the car traveling at a high rate of speed.

"Put your seat belt on Cammie," she said to a chorus of cars blowing horns as we whizzed by.

"What's going on?" I asked.

"Put your seat belt on."

Concerned, I snapped my belt in place. I looked at the digital speedometer. 98 mph.

"Why are you going so fast?!" I asked. "Slow down before you kill us!"

I looked again, 104 mph, 112 mph then 118 mph

"Let me out! Stop and let me out!"

I reached to open the app on my phone to press the emergency function. We hit a bump and the phone jumped out of my hand and slid under the seat.

"Cammie, this is my last trip." An agenda was in her voice.

"What? What do you mean?"

She jerked the car, switching us from the middle to the far left lane, the sped up faster.

128 mph, 133 mph, 140 mph. We were headed for a curve on an overpass.

I closed my eyes, screaming at the top of my lungs, "Stop the car!"

We hit the curve, smashed through the guardrail and over the bridge — but we didn't go down.

The car suspended like someone hit pause.

I was outside of my body, *looking* at my body.

It sounded like someone put my scream into a blender and made a muffled roar because my one voice became many.

I heard men, women and children screaming — but my scream was fear; theirs was joy.

One of my hands reached up and pulled my suspended frame back into itself. I blinked and everything was in real-time again.

"Bing," that familiar airline chime rang out.

I look down to see a boarding ticket upside down on my lap.

Flight 918 was written in its corner. I am back on the plane.

Everyone is waiting for me. John is standing there with my stepsons, Steve and Tanner. I turn around and see Chase, Dr. Mara, Dr. Jenny. We all embrace. My dear friend Glenda hugs me so tight I can't breathe. The homeless man I started with is now groomed; the priest is wearing the biggest smile, his hands wrapped in a rosary. My grandson, Bodhi, yells my name from the back, "MaiMai!" then runs into my arms. This feels like heaven. All my besties are here!

The copilot, Ms. Tina, motions for the plane to quiet and says a little prayer.

"Thank you for your power. Thank you for direction, protection and peace. Amen." When I open my eyes I see a group of mothers each holding pictures of their angels. They have all lost their children too. There is Staci from Arkansas, Angela from Kentucky, Tonya from Ohio, along with several others. All of us share the same story. All of us met at a DEA conference in Washington, D.C. We bonded first on the ground, and now in the air.

I settle back into seat 2-A. The lady next to me, the one who apologized on our previous leg, looks at me with the most comforting smile.

"Is this yours?" she asks, handing me my iPhone. "It slipped underneath the seat."

I offer a hesitant "thank you," mystified as to how she had it in her possession, but I have a bigger question.

"Where are we going next?" I ask.

"We're headed toward Purpose. The opioid epidemic will end. You've done a great job up here."

"Up here?" I ask.

"Yes, you've taken your journey well. Doing well up here,

means things go well down there. You never gave up and so the owner never gave up on you. As above, so below."

"Oh, wow," I respond. "One last question."

"Sure, Cammie."

"I met everyone on this flight. I know the owner, and I met the copilot, but who is flying the plane?"

She frowns, and seems confused. Her body language shifts to uneasy.

I ask again, this time in a whisper.

"Who is the pilot?"

Placing her hand on top of mine, she leans into my ear and says, "Wait — they never told you?"

SCAN HERE FOR MORE

EPILOGUE

ROGER ALAN WOLF II
April 22, 1968 - May 3, 2021

SCAN HERE FOR MORE

ACKNOWLEDGMENTS

I would like to thank GOD, first and foremost, and my beloved
angel spirits leading the way: my son Christopher, mother,
Charla and brother, Roger.

My husband, my love . . . my rock and best friend, John.

Chase and Tori, for blessing me with my grandson, Bodhi
Christopher, cheering me on and always telling me
"You got this."
A special thank you to my stepsons, Tanner and Steve, for
always being there, and to the entire Rice family for embracing
my boys and me from day one.

Appreciation to my parents, grandparents and
great-grandparents for showing me unconditional love.

To all my family and friends (you know who you are)
who continue to love me throughout my journey.
You all are my everything!

My grandma Tina, my copilot, my spiritual guide, I couldn't have done this without you.

To Scott and the CCF family in Cambodia, thank you for loving me on the hardest day of my life.

The entire Christopher Wolf Crusade team! You rock!

Thank you, Dennis Ross, for helping me put pen to paper in such an extraordinary way.

I love you with all my heart,
Cammie

RESOURCE LIBRARY

Find Treatment, Recovery Resources, Family Resources, Crisis
Support Hotline, Harm Reduction & Overdose Response, Signs of
Addiction, Wellness Skills, Related Media, Cammie's Playlist,
The CWC Crusade, Care Coach.

SCAN HERE FOR MORE

Cammie & baby
Christopher

Cammie's favorite photo
of her and Christopher

Christopher & Srey Nich,
the last photo taken of
Christopher

Christopher
graduates college!

Cammie with her
niece Bailey, Lexi
& her hero Scott
with kiddos

Cammie &
John with their
sponsored
CCF girls, Dalin
& SreyVin.

Cammie's kids at
the Cambodia
Rice Academy

Cammie receives an award from Usher's New Look with Usher & Sugar Ray Leonard

John speaking to UNL interns at General Electric

Usher's New Look Event!

Christopher's
funeral in
Cambodia

Cammie & Chase
saying goodbye

No words

Christopher's Hope Medical Clinic at
CCF in Cambodia

Ribbon cutting in Cambodia at the
CCF Christopher's Hope Medical Clinic

Cammie at the
DEA Summit

CwC Life Care
Specialist's
Research Team

A Blessed Day with the Pope

Cammie's Copilot, Grandma Tina

IN LOVING MEMORY

♥ Christopher ♥

In Loving Memory of Christopher Brett Wolf

Christopher's art, age 6

Christopher's art, age 18